CONCILIUM

Religion in the Seventies

CONCILIUM

Religion in the Seventies

EDITORIAL DIRECTORS: Edward Schillebeeckx (Dogma) •
Herman Schmidt (Liturgy) • Alois Müller (Pastoral) •
Hans Küng (Ecumenism) • Franz Böckle (Moral Theology) •
Johannes B. Metz (Church and World) • Roger Aubert (Church
History) • Teodoro Jiménez Urresti (Canon Law) • Christian
Duquoc (Spirituality) • Pierre Benoît and Roland Murphy
(Scripture)

CONSULTING EDITORS: Marie-Dominique Chenu • ✠Carlo
Colombo • Yves Congar • Andrew Greeley • Jorge Mejía •
Karl Rahner • Roberto Tucci

EXECUTIVE SECRETARY: (Awaiting new appointment),
Arksteestraat 3–5, Nijmegen, The Netherlands

Volume 80: Scripture

EDITORIAL BOARD: Bas van Iersel • Roland Murphy •
Luis Alonso Schökel • Josef Blank • Myles Bourke • Henri
Cazelles • Settimio Cipriani • Aelred Cody • José Croatto •
Jacques Dupont • Joseph Fitzmeyer • José-Marie González-Ruiz •
Lucas Grollenberg • Herbert Haag • Stanislas Lyonnet •
George MacRae • Martin McNamara • Salvador Muñoz Iglesias •
Franz Mussner • Angelo Penna • Kazimierz Romaniuk •
Heinrich Schlier • Rudolf Schnackenburg • Heinz Schürmann •
David Stanley • Francis Bruce Vawter • Anton Vögtle •
Thomas Worden • Silverio Zedda

OFFICE AND MINISTRY
IN THE CHURCH

Edited by

Bas van Iersel and
Roland Murphy

Herder and Herder

1972
HERDER AND HERDER NEW YORK
1221 Avenue of the Americas,
New York 10020

ISBN: 07–073610–3

Cum approbatione Ecclesiastica

Library of Congress Catalog Card Number: 72–3946

Printed in the United States

CONTENTS

PART III

DOCUMENTATION CONCILIUM

Editorial

The New Testament and the Present Crisis of the Ministry

WHY is our age discovering the New Testament ministries with fresh eyes and unprecedented interest? Part of the answer lies in the technical progress of exegesis, but more important are similarities in situation and problems.

I. ANALOGIES OR CONTRASTS?

Striking Similarities

Features which Catholicism used to regard as marginal have become the centre of attention. The New Testament ministries were at the service of small communities which were organized on a human scale and met in the house of a Christian (Acts 12. 12; 28. 30; Rom. 16. 5; 15. 19; 1 Cor. 16. 19; Col. 4. 15; Philem. 2), as today in Cuernavaca, Ponte de Carvalhos or elsewhere. The ministries did not yet have a clerical character; this is of interest in a period of declericalization. They did not even have a "priestly" character, and people have begun to ask if the error common to both Protestantism and Catholicism has not been to define the ministry in terms of priesthood, on the basis of *hierarchy* for the Catholics and on the *common* priesthood in the case of Luther. The suggestion is provocative, and makes a great deal of polemic seem superficial.

The last point around which new interest has grown is the delicate relations of sex and the sacred. No connection can be found in the New Testament between the ministry and celibacy, but rather the opposite, according to 1 Tim. 3. 2 and Tit. 1. 6, and this gives support to the present protests against this "law" as it exists in the Latin Church. Women took part in ministries of a diaconal type (Rom. 16. 1–3; cf. 6. 6, 12; Phil. 4. 2, 3) in this new society of which Paul claimed that it no longer recognized "male or female" (Gal. 3. 28), a striking challenge in the "uni-sex" age.

But smart parallels can be misleading, and we must take care not to fall into over-simplification or archaeologism. We should not decorate the origins of Christianity with modern fashions It is no longer possible today to write a new *Fabiola* or to dream of going back 2,000 years and ignoring a history to which the Holy Spirit has contributed so much. The aim of this issue is to define the scope and limits of the interest which is behind the present return to the sources on the question of the ministry.

A Contrast

It is first of all the contrast between the New Testament period and our own which strikes us so forcefully. One characteristic of the origins of Christianity was an amazing expansion of the new religion and the ministries; each of the little house groups of the primitive Church had its ministers, sometimes many of them.

Today, in contrast, priests are vanishing. This forecast by Ivan Illich, so amazing in 1967, has been steadily confirmed ever since. The decline has set in in every country of Europe and America, though at differing rates. Global expansion continues only in some countries in Asia (Vietnam, on the edge of the volcano, and India) and Africa (above all Tanzania and Uganda, but also Nigeria, though that is a special case). While the world population is increasing by about 200 million a year (7%), the number of Catholics is increasing by no more than 10,000,000, or less than 2%. (These figures are taken from the optimistic calculations of the Congregation for Education, which records a slight slowing down in the last two years.)

The number of priests has been falling since 1969, with a more rapid fall each year as a result of two related factors:

On the one hand, ordinations are becoming fewer and the

seminaries are emptying, which will produce a rapid reduction in manpower in 1975–76.

On the other hand, priests are leaving in increasing numbers. The Vatican statistical office records 13,440 cases between 1964 and 1970. To this should be added the departures during the last two years, 1971–72, which have increased, and, more important, departures without canonical authorization. This gives a total to date certainly over 20,000 (and according to Schallert this figure has been reached for the United States alone).

The number of priests in proportion to the number of Christians and the world's population is falling steadily year by year. In Italy the proportion has fallen from 1 priest per 350 inhabitants in 1901 to 1 per 1,900. For the world as a whole the ratio fell from 1 priest per 1,401 Catholics in 1966 to 1 per 1,535 in 1970. In Latin America the ratio is around 1:5,000, and the situation in that continent is such that the authorities no longer dare to make the calculation.[1]

The contrast between the present decline in the ministries and the expansion of the New Testament period invites us to a fundamental re-examination of the New Testament in order to rediscover Christ's purpose and the lessons of that exemplary situation in which "the Lord" did indeed "send out labourers into his harvest" (cf. Mt. 9. 37).

II. The True Lessons of the New Testament

Beyond Proof-Texts

Until recent years our reading of the Bible was determined by a situation solidly entrenched behind centuries of history. The ministries formed a priestly and hierarchical pyramid, pope-bishops-priests. The power of the pope included that of the bishops, and that of the bishops included that of the priests, and, at the bottom, the priests contained the laity, the non-priests, who had no power in canon law. What was chiefly sought from Scripture was a justification of these established forms. Anything beyond that was regarded as an historian's or archaeologist's hobby.

---

[1] A detailed table will be found in R. Laurentin, *Nouveaux ministères et fin du clergé, devant le troisième Synode* (Paris, 1971), pp. 79–100.

At the most, this past history was used as material for the meditations of those who received the full heritage of the past, symbolized by the major and minor orders, most of which they never exercised. The meaning of these symbolic functions came to be that the priest, possessor of power over the eucharistic body of Christ, embodied and recapitulated all the ministers of the past, as the development of the individual human embryo recapitulates the phylogenesis of the lower species. This grandiose structure was both simple and loaded.

It was simple in its pyramidal structure, because it recognized only one priestly ministry, the fullness of power over the eucharistic body of Christ, and restricted hierarchical differences to the order of government and authority: according to the most common schemas, it was in jurisdiction and not priesthood that the pope differed from the bishops and the bishops from the priests.

It was loaded because all the values of the past had been concentrated in the priest. As well as the orders of which the mind of the Church had kept a memory which now turns out to have been incomplete and particularly faulty with regard to the New Testament (the priest was doorkeeper, reader, acolyte, exorcist, subdeacon and deacon), there were the charismatic values. Most important of these were those of the monastic life, celibacy, the divine office and other obligations characteristic of religious, except poverty. The exception is amazing, because Christ made it one of his chief requirements for the ministers of the Gospel (Lk. 10. 4–5; cf. 9. 3–4, etc.). In sharp contrast, ordination was officially carried out to a "title", a title to an income, often from land, the title of an ecclesiastical benefice or a personal emolument. This omission revealed the failings of a system whose merit was to concentrate in "the priest" the weight of all the Christian demands and values. The fault was that it set up priests as a caste with a monopoly of all values, and in particular the possessions, knowledge and power of the Church, to the detriment of the laity, who were reduced to living on what remained. The disintegration of the structure shows the composite character already in evidence at Vatican II.

The new awareness of the relativity of the present has directed interest back to the New Testament. At the same time as the

Church is challenged, forced to look afresh at its future, it finds itself invited to look at its past, the further back as the crisis threatens to stretch forward ever further into the future: "The Church has eyes both in front and behind," St Bernard said. The uncertainty of the present forces us to look with fresh eyes at the past by destroying some of our prejudices. Until quite recently it was usual to identify (in a bold stroke of concordism) Christ's intentions with the juridical and theological constructions of the established situation. We realize today that Jesus did not institute either bishops or priests, in the ancient or the modern sense of the terms. What Christ handed on was not a canonical blueprint, but a living intention. He revealed love, *agape*, in his own person. His revelation was God-as-Love really spread and communicated among men. It was in the service of this gift that he formulated elements of doctrine and organization, especially the rites and services of *agape*. He established them in sharp contrast with the powers of this world: "The kings of the Gentiles exercise lordship over them; and those in authority over them are called benefactors. But not so with you; rather let the greatest among you become as the youngest, and the leader as one who serves" (Lk. 22. 25–27). The instruction was rooted in his example: "I am among you as one who serves" (Lk. 22. 27).

Origins and Creativity

In this way Jesus left the apostles great freedom to invent the structures and forms of their functions and of the succession. It is fascinating to trace their cautious experiments, often successful, to meet the needs of the communities (see Lemaire's article, pp. 35–49 below).

It is astonishing to see the freedom left to the apostles by Christ, dead and risen at the centre of a human failure, the authority, without a trace of paternalism, to give the Church its first structure. A striking sign of this freedom is the fact that the only forms of the ministry formally instituted by Christ were not continued by his disciples. The Twelve co-opted Matthias before Pentecost (Acts 1. 21–26), but thereafter they never again made up the number of the Twelve. Other forms were used to continue the essential functions, preaching and calling the people together, the forgiveness of sins, the Eucharist and the preservation of unity.

There is also no sign that the "seventy-two", whose sending out with extremely precise instructions from Christ is recorded in Luke 10. 1–12, were continued in that form. Nevertheless, this gospel pericope, more than any other, embodies the forms of imperative rules and canonical norms laying down not only the style and language of preaching but prohibiting the carrying of a purse and luggage and specifying how they should travel, lodge, and so on.

The ministries which flourished in such profusion in the early Church, including those which took over from the apostles, thus seem to have been largely "functional" creations under the pressure of events and the inspiration of the Holy Spirit. This is clearly true of the first ministry where we know anything of the origin, the "seven", whom historians have for so long identified with the later deacons. Chosen "to serve tables" (Acts 6. 1–3), they went considerably beyond the ministry entrusted to them for the purpose of allowing the apostles to devote themselves "to prayer and to the ministry of the word". The seven in their turn devoted themselves to preaching, more outspokenly than the apostles, and the vehemence of their prophetic language involved the Church in the cycle of persecutions which carried it to the ends of the earth.

The New Ministries of Today

This creativity of the primitive Church in the service of Christ among living communities corresponds to the aspirations of our own time. We are not simply in a period of decline. The disintegration of the clergy, and above all the crisis of identity which makes it impossible for so many people to adopt existing clerical and administrative forms, are in fact, in many ways, the reverse of a positive phenomenon, the birth of new ministries.

(1) As the seminaries decline, a new type of vocation is developing outside the seminaries, no longer among children who are turned into clerics but among adults, no longer among solitaries, marginal by vocation, but among men with a place in society, formed by a career, who cannot conceive of their service except as that of whole men. This situation brings us closer to the choice of ministers in the New Testament.

(2) In "basic communities" and informal groups, services and

functions are growing up organically, in a way not unlike that of the New Testament period. These spontaneous growths are also very varied, recalling the irrepressible pluralism of the earliest centuries. The ministries springing up among the Pentecostals (including the Catholics) are very different from those growing up in Latin American grassroots communities or in informal groups in Italy, and it is too early to say what will take root. Already, however, the re-emergence of lay ministers (community leaders in Africa and East Berlin) was one of the points which attracted most attention at the 1971 episcopal synod.

(3) The diaconate is developing, slowly and with difficulty, most probably because its restoration was conceived too much in a spirit of archaeologism and too often carried out as part of an administrative scheme; administrative preoccupations absorbed the charismatic movement which appeared in Germany and later in France on the eve of the Council. Nevertheless, the number of deacons has increased in geometric progression since the first ordinations on 28 April 1968: 150 at the end of 1970, 339 in 1971 and more than twice the latter figure already in 1972.[2]

(4) Women, who during the last few centuries virtuously recoiled from sometimes urgent vocations to the presbyteral ministry,[3] are now looking for ways to fulfil these aspirations, and groups are forming with this aim in mind. The administrative need to fill so many empty posts has also led to women religious being given (without ordination) the duties of parish priests: the celebrations of marriages and funerals, preaching, the conduct of Sunday worship including the distribution of the Eucharist, in other words all the functions of a deacon without exception and all the functions of a priest except saying Mass, hearing con-

[2] "Etat des diacres dans le monde", in *Effort diaconal*, 2 rue Jean Carriès, 69 Lyon, France, 26 (May–June 1972), p. 22, and additional information supplied by *Pro Mundi Vita*. Deacons are an essentially European and North American phenomenon: in 1971 there were 188 in Europe, 135 in America and only 14 in Africa, 1 in Asia and 1 in Australia. There were 2,000 volunteers for the diaconate in the world as a whole, with the highest figures in the U.S.A. (430) and Belgium (150).

[3] R. Laurentin, *Marie, l'Eglise et le sacerdoce* (Paris, 1953), 1, pp. 423–7, where details are given of the cases of Caroline Clément (1842–46), Teresa of the Child Jesus, Marie Antoinette de Geuser and others. An international association, *L'Amicale des femmes aspirant au ministère presbytéral*, was set up privately in June 1972.

fessions and anointing the sick; and some of these women have even been given the duties of episcopal vicars, in Detroit and Rio de Janeiro, for example.

(5) Finally, the number of theology students is increasing as the seminaries empty, which reflects to an inner rebirth of the charism of doctor or teacher, in forms very different from those which can be discerned in the New Testament. In Germany, the leading country in this field, the number of students has risen from 4,874 in 1957 to 5,544 in 1967, half of whom are lay people. In Paris a much more recent development has increased the number of students at the Instituts de Théologie from a few hundred to over 2,000.

The Situational Analogy

At the starting-point of these convergences a number of situational analogies can be found. In the New Testament period as in our own, a vast pagan world offered unprecedented opportunities of communication, an extraordinary mixing of cultures, intense and sometimes anxious inquiry about the meaning of human life, vigorous religious movements and the need for a genuine experience of life in community. In the New Testament period as today crisis and change provoked creativity. The New Testament is an example of the predominance of movement over system which is a widely proclaimed goal today.

The period of the New Testament had also undergone the most radical experience of declericalization ever seen; this was characteristic of the transition from the Old Testament to the New. The Jewish Church in Jerusalem had seen "a great number of the (Jewish) priests (*hiereis*)" adopt the faith (Acts 6. 7), and these lost their priestly identity on entering a community in which the ministers were definitely not *hiereis*. This situation had deep roots. Jesus himself had been legally a layman; it was as a layman that he had spoken in his village synagogue (Lk. 4. 16–17) and pursued his whole career as a prophet (Mt. 13. 57; 21. 11, 46), increasingly separate from the old priesthood and its temple. The Twelve were also laymen, and so were the ministers of the new community, the *episkopoi* and *presbyteroi*, whom the New Testament never describes as priests (*hiereis-sacerdotes*). The only basis for an objection to this view is the symbolic passage in which Paul describes the ministry of the word as a "priestly service" (Rom. 15. 16; cf. 12. 1).[4]

The New Testament period, like our own time, marks a break with the idea of the sacred characterized by taboos attached to material things, religious buildings and times or persons set apart. Although Christ (cf. Mk. 15. 29, 38; Jn. 2. 19), and more clearly his disciples (Acts 7. 13–14, 47–9; 17. 24; Heb. 9. 11, 24; cf. 2 Cor. 5. 1), were condemned for rejecting the material temple in favour of a temple of living stones, the old form of the sacred (equated with the golden calf by Stephen in Acts 7) was reconstructed in the course of the centuries, and it is difficult even today to transcend it definitively. Six years after Vatican II, during which it was emphasized again and again that the whole people of God is consecrated, the draft of the new canon law (rejected or criticized by so many episcopates) still makes a contrast between "the ministers of the Church", who are "sacred", and the laity who are not (Canon 27; cf. 14; 18; 29 §3; 31, etc.). The New Testament points the way to a purification and a transcendence which would not be a negation of the sacred but a sacralization of life itself from within, in the living body of Christ (see J. Colson's article).

This basic New Testament attitude helps us to understand the new branches of study developing today.

Functionalism

The first and most important lesson is that the ministries of the New Testament are functional; their objects are determined by the service of the community and not by the internal aims of a bureaucratic apparatus. In the New Testament, these objects take priority over *a priori* rules, and the impulses of the Spirit are more important than administrative convenience, even if the impulses of the Spirit as they affect the ministry require control, as can be seen from Paul's intervention in Corinth (1 Cor. 11–14). The need is not to exclude authority or to see that it is exercised in the name of Christ, but to see it as a function of faith, which

[4] On the limits of the priestly vocabulary in Rom. 15. 16 see C. Weiner, "Hierourgein", in *Studiorum Paulinorum Congressus 1961*, 12 (Rome, 1963), pp. 393–401; and "Excursis 1", in *Les Prêtres*, Unam Sanctam 68 (Paris, 1968), pp. 257–9.

gives the communities their internal structure like the life-force in living organisms.

Dedication to Mission

Another important hint to be found in the New Testament is that ministries are fundamentally missionary. At the beginning and throughout the period of expansion the itinerant ministers took precedence over the resident, the "apostles" over the *presbyteroi* and *episkopoi* whom they appointed locally. So Paul mentions first of all "apostles, prophets and evangelists", before "pastors and teachers" (Eph. 4. 11–13; Rom. 12. 6–8). Both Paul's and Peter's were essentially travelling ministries and, if they had not been, neither apostle would have reached Rome, where martyrdom put an accidental end to their missionary journeys.

The progress of the mission is not to be measured by the growth of organization or by increasing numbers of workers (though numbers are important, see Acts 2. 41, 47; 4. 4; 5. 14, etc.). The measure is that "the word of the Lord increased" as the refrain in Acts puts it (Acts 6. 7; 12. 24; 19. 20). The similarities should not be pressed, but we must nevertheless admit that the analogies between the primitive situation and that of today have renewed our awareness of Christ's intentions.

III. The Articles

This biblical issue, the last to appear before the inter-disciplinary reorganization of *Concilium*, is transitional, in that it approaches the question of the ministries by confronting the New Testament data (the subject of the first four articles) with the events of the present (Bulletin and Documentation), taking in some key moments in the history of the Church's life and teaching. Our intention is not to repeat what has been said in other issues about the ministry in the New Testament,[5] but to grasp the changing situation of the Church.

[5] In particular no reference has been made to the article by John McKenzie, in *Concilium*, April 1972 (American edn., vol. 74). Within the context of an ecumenical issue devoted to mutual recognition of ecclesial ministries, this article showed that the original pluralism and the unfinished state in which the Twelve left the ministries leave considerable scope for ecumenical agreement,

1. *The New Testament Model*

The New Testament shows this situation to be primarily not a finished product, but more like the development of organisms (Schnider's and Stenger's article), diverse and experimental; the latter point is brought out by Lemaire's article on the gestation of the first ministries. This pluralism, used for their own purposes by the Constantinian period and the Middle Ages, may inspire further developments on an ecumenical scale, to meet specific needs (Kearney's article), especially the existential search for the sacred (Colson).

2. *The Lessons of History*

Three articles describe the barrier which has arisen over the centuries between us and the ministries of the New Testament. Both in doctrine (Fransen) and attempts at reform (Ganoczy), the anxiety to give permanence or reinforcement to established ministries allowed hierarchical power to dominate the missionary drive. The process is not irreversible, as can be seen from the attempt of Vatican II to restructure everything in order to base the ministries on the word, and from the original effort within the Anglican Communion to base the theology of the episcopate on mission, while retaining, in a marginal position, the legal and hierarchical functions associated with this office (Bishop Neill's article).

This is a crucial problem, how to preserve the original inspiration of the Gospel in the midst of administrative and legal requirements and political interference. How can we prevent ministries from being absorbed into the category of powers?

3. *The Issues of Today*

All this points to the need for a fresh look at the present situation.

Where have women got to in their aspirations to ecclesial ministries at a time when the only places in which they are denied responsible positions are the Paris Bourse and the Roman Church (Joan Brothers' article)? What is the general situation revealed by the many inquiries carried out before the Synod among priests of different countries and practically ignored so far (Kerkhofs)?

Finally, what are the results of the latest discussion on the problems thus raised (Houdijk)?

In the midst of a crisis full of both dangers and promises, it is our hope that the inter-disciplinary studies in this issue of *Concilium* may sharpen the sight of a Church with "eyes both in front and behind", so that the example and teaching of the Good Shepherd may, by the ever-living power of the Spirit, bring forth new charisms for the service of the eucharistic community within which the body of Christ grows with its mysterious growth.

RENÉ LAURENTIN

Translated by Francis McDonagh

PART I
ARTICLES

Franz Schnider/Werner Stenger

The Church as a Building and the Building up of the Church

Static and Dynamic Features in a Set of Images of the Church

I. JESUS CHRIST: THE FOUNDATION OF THE CHURCH (1 Cor. 3. 9–17)

1. *Laying the Foundation and building upon it*

In 1 Cor. 3. 9 Paul says of the church at Corinth that it is God's field and God's building,[1] meaning that it is the property of God. The verse contains two sentences, in which Paul speaks with the aid of two sets of images of his work and that of Apollos in the church. This is necessary, because Paul sees the existence of the

[1] A selected bibliography on the topics discussed. Y. M. J. Congar, *Le mystère du Temple*; B. Gaertner, *The Temple and the Community in Qumran and the New Testament* (SNTS Monograph Series 1, Cambridge, 1965); G. Klinzing, "Die Umdeutung des Kultus in der Qumrangemeinde und im Neuen Testament" (StUNT 7) (Göttingen, 1971); R. J. McKelvey, *The New Temple* (Oxford, 1969); O. Michel, "Naos" in *Theologisches Wörterbuch zum Neuen Testament*, IV, cols. 884–95; art. "Oikos, etc.", *Theologisches Wörterbuch zum Neuen Testament*, V, cols. 122–61; F. Mussner, "Beiträge aus Qumran zum Verständnis des Epheserbriefes" in *Praesentia Salutis* (Düsseldorf, 1967), pp. 197–207; F. Mussner, *Christus das All und die Kirche* (Trierer Theol. Studien 5, Trier, 2nd edn. 1968); J. Pfammatter, "Die Kirche als Bau", *Anal. Greg.* 110 (Rome, 1960); J. Ratzinger, *Volk und Haus Gottes in Augustinus Lehre von der Kirche* (Münchener Theol. Studien II, 7, Munich, 1954); H. Schlier, "Zu den Namen der Kirche in den Paulinischen Briefen", in *Besinnung auf das Neuen Testament* (2nd edn., Freiburg, 1964), pp. 294–306; R. Schnackenburg, *Die Kirche im Neuen Testament* (Quaestiones Disputatae 14; 3rd edn., Freiburg, 1961), pp. 140–6; P. Vielhauer, *Oikodome* (Karlsruhe and Durlach, 1940); H. Wenschkewitz, *Die Spiritualisierung der Kultusbegriffe Tempel, Priester und Opfer im Neuen Testament* (*Angelos*, Beiheft 4, Leipzig, 1932).

parties which have come into being in Corinth as a threat to the unity of the church (cf. 1 Cor. 1. 10–17).[2] This association of the two sets of images, planting and the building of a house, was anticipated in the Old Testament and in secular Greek writing.[3]

As work which was essential in the conditions of life at that period[4] the planting of a vineyard and the building of a house excused a person from military service (Deut. 20. 5–7). According to Jer. 18. 7–10, it is God who plucks up and breaks down, builds and plants. He sets the prophet over the nations to carry out this activity (Jer. 1. 10). In the eschatological period especially, God will watch over his people to build up and to plant (Jer. 31. 28; cf. Jer. 24. 6; Isa. 60. 21). Paul's primary purpose, however, is not to set out ecclesiological doctrine. He is seeking to mediate and bring clarity into the dispute between the members of the church who appeal to him or to Apollos. For what are Apollos and Paul? They are servants of the church, through whom the church came to believe. Since both are servants, there is no distinction between them. There is a difference only between the nature of their service (1 Cor. 3. 4 f.). Paul planted, whereas Apollos watered (1 Cor. 3. 6). The person who plants begins; the person who waters continues. Paul founded the church of Corinth (Acts 18. 1–17) and Apollos preached in the church that he founded (Acts 19. 1). But the difference in the form of service does not imply any order of rank between the servants which could give rise to the forming of parties, for it is God who gave the growth (1 Cor. 3. 6 f.). The primary purpose of the second set of images is the same. Like a skilled master builder Paul laid the foundation of the building of God which is the church, while another man continued building upon it (v. 10). If the image were to be continued in strict analogy to the first set of images, one would have to say that the master builder

---

[2] On the parties in Corinth cf. W. Schmithals, *Die Gnosis in Korinth* (FRLANT 66, 2nd edn., Göttingen, 1965); D. Georgi, *Die Gegner des Paulus im 2. Korintherbrief* (WMANT 11, Neukirchen, 1964).

[3] Cf. A. Fridrichsen, *Ackerbau und Hausbau in formelhaften Wendungen in der Bibel und bei Platon* (Neutest. Forschungen, Sonderheft der ThStKr, Stuttgart, 1922), pp. 185 f.; cf. also J. Pfammatter, *op. cit.*, pp. 19 f.

[4] Cf. H. Conzelmann, *Der erste Brief an die Korinther* (Meyer Kommentare 5, Göttingen, 1969), p. 94.

who laid the foundation and the other person who continued building, for all the difference in their service, are as servants nothing, because it is God who sets up and maintains the whole building.

2. The Apostolic Gospel of Jesus Christ as the Foundation of the Church's Doctrine

But the analogy between the images is not carried through,[5] since Paul turns to consider more closely than before the difference between the kinds of service the two carried out. For Paul's self-consciousness as an apostle, his knowledge that he was the founder of a church was of particular importance. According to Rom. 15. 20 he made it his ambition to preach the gospel only where Christ had not yet been named, in order not to build on another man's foundation. This was not, however, an ambition to be a pioneer in new territory. Rather, Paul knows that it is his task "to be a minister of Christ Jesus to the Gentiles" (Rom. 15. 16), a grace given to him by God (Rom. 15. 15). In his service the promise that "they shall see who have never been told of him" (Rom. 15. 21; Isa. 52. 15; cf. Gal. 1. 7 f.) is eschatologically fulfilled. The fact that he has also laid the foundation in Corinth is part of his "reason to be proud" as an apostle (Rom. 15. 17). It is his own specific grace, given to him by God (v. 15).

But in this consciousness of his apostolic calling, by which, for all his previous emphasis upon unity, Paul knows that he differs from Apollos, there is also an element of fear, which leads him to lay more emphasis upon the difference between his activity in founding the church and that of others, who continued the building of the church.[6] In v. 11 he explicitly states that no other foundation can be laid in place of that which is laid already. The close connection between v. 11 and v. 10 shows that the warning to subsequent preachers in the church, "let each man take care how he builds upon it" (v. 10), which already departs from the original purpose of the statement, conceals Paul's fear that "building

---

[5] For the way the imagery is used, cf. P. Vielhauer, op. cit., pp. 83 f.; W. Straub, Die Bildersprache des Apostels Paulus (Tübingen, 1937).

[6] The fact that the name of Apollos is no longer mentioned must not necessarily be seen as an attack on the party of Cephas (as in P. Vielhauer, op. cit., p. 182).

upon it" may consist not merely of building upon the foundation, but may take the form of a building which does not take
the foundation into account or which is even erected on a new
foundation. Here, then, "laying the foundation" has a meaning
which goes beyond the analogy of "planting". The fixed and
permanent foundation is Jesus Christ (v. 11). But what is actually
meant by this?

The metaphorical expressions of the laying of foundations and
building upon them is attested in the style of the Stoic diatribe.[7]
But the term "foundation", in association with "building",
"temple" and "planting" is also found in the Qumran texts (all
three terms together in 1 QS 8. 4–8). On the other hand, a literal
parallel to the building upon the foundation is not attested in the
Qumran writings.[8] Paul begins by using the Hellenistic metaphor
of the laying of a foundation and building upon it[9] and only
when he comes to use the image of the temple (v. 16) does he
approach the eschatological conceptions of Qumran expressed in
the images of the foundation and the temple.[10] The foundation is
what exists before anyone can build upon it. It cannot be changed
and no *other* foundation can be laid (v. 11). The laying of the
foundation took place in the apostle's preaching of the gospel
which founded the church. The apostle's gospel is therefore the
norm laid down for any further preaching in the church. Is this
foundation Jesus Christ in person, or teaching about him?[11] The
gospel of Christ preached by the apostle is both the gospel concerning Christ and the gospel in which Christ proclaims himself.[12] That no other (*allon*) foundation can be laid instead of or
in addition to (*para*) what has been laid means therefore that no
other gospel can be preached besides that which the apostle
preached in founding the church.

Thus v. 11 is closely connected in both terminology and content with Gal. 1. 6–9 and 2 Cor. 11. 4. In Gal. 1. 6 Paul expresses
his astonishment that the Galatians are deserting God, who called

[7] H. Conzelmann, *op. cit.*, p. 93, with references.
[8] Cf. G. Klinzing, *op. cit.*, p. 170.
[9] Cf. P. Vielhauer, *op. cit.*, p. 86.
[10] Cf. G. Klinzing, *op. cit.*, pp. 168–72.
[11] Cf. J. Pfammatter, *op. cit.*, pp. 25 f.
[12] Cf. H. Schlier, *Wort Gottes* (Rothenfelser Reihe 4, Würzburg, 1958),
pp. 350–52.

them in the grace of Christ, and turning to a different (*heteron*) gospel. This calling by God took place in the apostle's preaching of the gospel. This gospel is the norm, and by comparison with it this other (*allo*) gospel is not a gospel at all (Gal. 1. 7). *The apostle himself is bound by it*; not even an angel from heaven may preach a gospel "contrary to", "instead of", "in addition to" (*par'ho*)[13] what the apostle preached in founding the Galatian church (Gal. 1. 8 f.). This gospel is Paul's norm because it was not received from a man, but through the revelation of Jesus Christ (Gal. 1. 12) which God let him experience on the way to Damascus (Gal. 1. 16). The Galatians, in Paul's view, are turning away from his gospel by returning to the observation of the law as a way of salvation (Gal. 4. 9 f., 21), expressed in their intention of having themselves circumcised (Gal. 5. 1–4). With regard to the Galatian situation, therefore, the specific content of the unchangeable apostolic gospel is the message of the freedom from the law and of justification by faith. This does not mean that the preachers who are preaching in Corinth another (*allon*) Jesus and a different (*heteron*) gospel from that of Paul (2 Cor. 11. 4)—like the Galatian false teachers—were trying to bring the church back to observe the law and the way of salvation. But the gospel of freedom from the law and justifying faith, which Paul wants to impress once again upon the Galatians, is merely the practical consequence of the heart of the Pauline gospel, Jesus Christ, publicly portrayed as crucified before the eyes of the Galatians (Gal. 3. 1). In the light of the scripture: "Cursed be everyone who hangs on a tree" (Gal. 3. 13; Deut. 21. 23) Paul recognized Jesus as the one who "redeemed us from the curse of the law, having become a curse for us (on the cross)" (Gal. 3. 13). It is the crucified and risen Christ who supplies and guarantees the Spirit to the Galatians (Gal. 3. 5). This also justifies the interpretation of 2 Cor. 11. 4 in this sense. For the preaching of another Jesus and a different gospel forms a parallel to the reception of a Spirit different from the one the Corinthians received in Paul's preaching of the gospel which founded their church. Without deciding upon the question of the form of doctrine taught by the false teachers in Corinth whom Paul mentions, we may say that "the

[13] H. Schlier, *Der Brief an die Galater* (Meyer Kommentare 7, Göttingen, 1962), p. 40.

other gospel", "the other Jesus", who bestows the "different Spirit" (2 Cor. 11. 4) is not in fact the Jesus Christ of the Pauline gospel who died and rose again to atone for our sins and who was preached amongst the Corinthians by Paul (2 Cor. 1. 19). The same, therefore, is also true of the foundation of 1 Cor. 3. 11, which cannot be replaced by any other—it is the Jesus Christ who is preached in Paul's gospel. Jesus Christ, who died on the cross to atone "for our sins" and rose again, constitutes the church, in and through the apostolic gospel, and permanently determines the doctrine built upon that gospel.

The apostle's gospel of Jesus Christ is therefore both the foundation and the norm for all further preaching and teaching in the Church. The mention of more or less valuable building materials, which those who build upon the foundation can use (v. 12), refers to qualitative distinctions in the kind of building.[14] The qualitative distinctions of doctrine derive from the greater or lesser conformity of the doctrine of the "post-apostolic" preachers with the gospel that lays the foundation. In so far as they build upon the foundation, the different quality of their work will be revealed in the judgment at the end of time (v. 13), but they themselves will be saved (v. 15). In this respect the preachers mentioned in vv. 14 and 15 are contrasted to him who in v. 17 destroys "God's temple". Whereas they may be rewarded or punished, but will in any case be saved in the end, he who destroys God's temple will be destroyed.

3. Jesus Christ the Foundation of the Temple of the Church

The relationship between those who build upon the foundation of the apostolic gospel and anyone who destroys God's temple enables us to take the "destruction of the temple" similarly as a form of "post-apostolic" preaching, one which does not, however, build upon the foundation. That is, it preaches a doctrine which is not in accordance with the apostolic gospel. Paul does not, however, say that the foundation, the gospel, is destroyed,

---

[14] The interpretation which sees in the various building materials images for the different degrees of commitment or the moral qualities of the preachers who carry on the building isolates the verses from the context of the whole set of images. Studies of attempts at this kind of solution: J. Gnilka, Ist 1 Cor. 3. 10–15 ein Schriftzeugnis für das Fegefeuer? (Düsseldorf, 1955), and J. Pfammatter, op. cit., pp. 29 f.

but speaks of the destruction of the temple, by introducing in v. 16 a new image, which he likewise relates to the image of the foundation in v. 11, that of the Church as God's temple. Anyone trying to replace the foundation, the apostolic gospel of Jesus Christ, also destroys God's temple, the Church. Thus the apostolic gospel of Jesus Christ is both the foundation for the "post-apostolic" *doctrine* and also the foundation of the *Church community*.

The description of the community as God's temple characterizes it as the eschatological temple expected by Judaism when the end came (Isa. 28. 16 f.; Enoch 91. 13; Jubilees 1. 17), and in which God would dwell for ever (cf. 2 Cor. 6. 16–18).[15] The Church is God's temple, because the Spirit of God dwells in it. In the same way, every individual, because he belongs to this church, is also the temple of this holy Spirit (1 Cor. 6. 19). The Qumran community also understood itself as the temple (1 QS 5. 5 f.; 8. 5), but also as the foundation as well (1 QS 7. 17; 9. 3). In 1 QS 8. 5 the terms "a holy house for Israel" and "a foundation of the Holy of Holies for Aaron" are in parallel to each other and both refer to the community (cf. 1 QS 5. 5 f.).[16] "Foundation" is synonymous, as *pars pro toto*, with the "holy house", i.e., the temple. The community is both the temple and the foundation. It is not the foundation of an eschatological temple which has still to be built, but even now, in place of the temple of Jerusalem, it is at once the foundation and the true eschatological temple for Israel. Paul, however, makes a distinction between the foundation and the temple. The foundation is not the community itself, but Jesus Christ. The community is the eschatological temple only because Jesus Christ is its foundation. How is this? The context of 1 QS 8. 6 f. (cf. 1 QS 5. 6) shows that by referring to itself as "temple" and "foundation" the community is expressing its consciousness of "atoning for the land" at the present day[17] (1 QS 8. 6; cf. 1 QS 5. 6) and "giving the godless retribution for their deeds" in the future judgment[18] (1 QS 8. 7; cf. 1 QS 5. 6 f.).

The idea of atonement is also found in Paul in association with

[15] Cf. O. Michel, "Naos", in *Theologishes Wörterbuch*, IV, cols. 890 f.
[16] Cf. J. Klinzing, *op. cit.*, p. 51.
[17] *Ibid., op. cit.*, p. 57.   [18] *Ibid.*

the image of the foundation, but because he does not relate the foundation collectively to the community of the Church, but individually to Jesus Christ who was crucified for us the Church itself does not carry out the eschatological atonement. It participates in it through faith. The temple is the place of the presence of God and the place in which the sacrifice of atonement is offered. The community can be the place where God is present and the eschatological sacrifice is offered because the foundation of the temple of the community is the crucified and risen Christ. As the crucified Christ, he is the eschatological sacrifice (Gal. 3. 13) and, as the one who died for us, he gives the eschatological gift of the Spirit (Gal. 3. 5, 14). Thus the Church is not the temple of God in itself and does not guarantee in itself the presence of the *eschaton*. It can be described as eschatological only in so far as it participates in the *eschaton* which took place and continues to take place in Jesus Christ. The image of the community as the temple must not be understood as a portrayal of the Church as an already finished and completed building. All that is complete is the eschatological foundation, Jesus Christ.

Paul therefore assumes that the foundation he has laid will be built upon. He knows that even he must go on building up the churches he has founded through the whole of his apostolic activity (2 Cor. 10. 8; 13. 10). In other passages in Paul where we find the image of the temple referring to the individual (1 Cor. 6. 19) or to the community (2 Cor. 6. 16) without any mention at the same time of the foundation which is distinguished from it, the paraenetic context[19] shows that the Church is not being considered from the point of view of its existing perfection, but is being exhorted to become what it basically already is through its foundation Jesus Christ,[20] the holy temple of God.

II. Apostles and Prophets as the Foundation of the Church and Christ Jesus as the Corner-stone (Eph. 2. 20–22)

1. *The Foundation and Corner-stone as Norms*

We find in Eph. 2. 20–22 a complexity of images from the set "building—foundation—temple" very like that in 1 Cor. 3. 9–17,

---

[19] Cf. P. Vielhauer, *op. cit.*, p. 86.
[20] Cf. H. Conzelmann, *op. cit.*, p. 97.

which was applied primarily to the concrete situation of the community in Corinth, and was developed only secondarily as an ecclesiological reflection. By contrast, in Eph. 2. 19–22, the images are used primarily as a reflection about the universal Church.[21] The historical situation of the Church had changed when this letter was written. The transition from the apostolic to the post-apostolic period was accompanied by a change of perspective, which can be perceived in a shift in the images used.[22] Verse 20 describes the Gentile Christians as having been "built upon the foundation of the apostles and prophets". Although the terminology is the same as in 1 Cor. 3. 10 ff. (*epoikodomein, themelion*) the ideas expressed are clearly different. The expression "foundation of the apostles and prophets" does not mean, as in 1 Cor. 3. 10, the foundation *laid* by the apostles and prophets, but the foundation which the apostles and prophets *are*.[23] Those addressed in the letter are built upon this foundation. Thus, in contract to 1 Cor. 3. 11, the foundation is not Jesus Christ but the group of the apostles and prophets.

To whom does this refer? According to Eph. 3. 5, to them has been revealed the eschatological mystery that "the Gentiles are fellow heirs, members of the same body, and partakers of the promise in Christ Jesus through the gospel". Thus they have received revelation for the purposes of enabling the Gentiles too to share in eschatological salvation by belonging to the Church. Eph. 3. 3 shows that Paul is also included in this group. He too

[21] Cf. J. Gnilka, "Das Kirchenmodell des Epheserbriefes, *Bibl. Zeitschrift* 15 (1971), pp. 163–73; F. Mussner, *Christus das All und die Kirche*, p. 110.

[22] H. Schlier, *Der Brief and die Epheser* (3rd cdn., Düsseldorf, 1962), p. 142 f., also speaks of a shift in the point of view, but because he maintains the Pauline authorship attributes it to a "continuous process of clarification" (p. 143), which this train of thought underwent in the "consciousness" (p. 142) of the apostle. But the true significance of the differences between 1 Cor. 3. 9–17 and Eph. 2. 20–22 appears only when the Epistle to the Ephesians is seen as a product of the Church's second generation. A consideration of the transition from the apostolic to the post-apostolic periods has important hermeneutic consequences for other passages beside the present one. Cf. H. Hegermann, "Der geschichtliche Ort der Pastoralbriefe", in *Theologische Versuche* II (Berlin, 1970), pp. 47–63.

[23] Cf. F. Mussner, *Christus das All und die Kirche*, p. 108; J. Pfammatter, *op. cit.*, pp. 83 f.

has a special relationship with the Gentiles. He is the prisoner of Christ Jesus for them (*hyper hymōn*); through him and his suffering as a prisoner (cf. Col. 1. 24), in which he shares in the representative suffering of Jesus, the salvation which Jesus' suffering has obtained reaches the Gentiles. Thus "apostles and prophets" are seen as being related in a special way to the Gentiles. Through their ministry the gospel is proclaimed amongst the Gentiles so that they can come to the Church. Because the apostles and prophets have received revelation for the purpose of winning the Gentiles for the Church, one can see in the expression "the apostles and prophets" a general term for the first generation of Christian preachers through whom the Church moved from Judaism to universality.

There is little point in trying to make a more precise distinction between the tasks of the apostles and the prophets. There is no consideration here of the difference between their ministries. The "prophets" are not Old Testament prophets, but prophets of the early Church (cf. Eph. 3. 5; 4. 11).[24] Nor does the term "the apostles" refer specifically to the twelve apostles,[25] but in general to the authoritative preachers of the first generation. According to Ephesians, their important function is that they have taken the step towards the universal mission. In so far as the generation which founded the Church brought about the universality of the Church, it was the foundation for the Gentile Christians who in the next generation, represented by the Epistle to the Ephesians, built upon them. The "early Church" mediated the eschatological salvation present in Jesus to the Church formed from the nations. In so far as the universal spread of salvation is a feature of the *eschata*, the early Church is itself eschatological in nature. In it the bounds set, at least in practice, by the fact that Jesus' ministry took place in Israel, are broken.

But have we not here a contradiction to 1 Cor. 3. 11, where Jesus Christ is called the foundation?[26] One must remember that

[24] Cf. H. Schlier, *Epheserbrief*, p. 142; J. Pfammatter, *op. cit.*, pp. 87–97; J. Gnilka, *Der Epheserbrief* (Herders theologischer Kommentar zum NT X, 2, Freiburg, 1971), p. 157.

[25] Cf. J. Gnilka, *Epheserbrief*, p. 157.

[26] J. Gnilka (*Epheserbrief*, p. 156) regards it as unnecessary to look for "a reconciliation of this difference". The difference is in substance "unimportant, since the essential function of Christ in Ephesians is described

in 1 Cor. 3. 10 f. Paul emphasizes that he, the apostle, laid the foundation. From the point of view of the post-apostolic Church, what the apostle did here, and his person, are seen as one and the same. For the apostle himself to lay the foundation was the gift of God's grace to him personally, and was part of the event of salvation. To this extent the post-apostolic Church had a theological right to understand the apostle himself as a foundation, especially as the idea of Jesus Christ as the one foundation of the Church is not overlooked, but is asserted in Eph. 2. 20–22 in an image of a different kind.[27]

In 1 Cor. 3. 9–17 the apostle's gospel of the crucified and risen Christ was both the foundation of the Church and also the norm for the Church and for the doctrine which was built upon it. The foundation bore the walls built upon it, and gave its form to these walls. When in Eph. 2. 20 the apostles and prophets are called the foundation, do they as such take over the double function of the foundation in 1 Cor. 3. 9–17? Are they seen as the foundation which *founds* the Church and provides its further *norm*?[28] They are certainly its founders. The universal Church rests upon the foundation of the apostles and prophets, its founders. In contrast to 1 Cor. 3. 9–17, only the universal aspect is emphasized in Eph. 2. 20–22. But are the apostles and prophets the permanent norm for the Church and does the form of the foundation also determine the form of the building set upon it? The answer does not simply follow from the image of the foundation.

We must consider its connection with another element in the

---

differently in the imagery of building in Ephesians". But this inquiry in fact makes particularly clear the differences between the apostolic and the post-apostolic points of view, and the continuity of the apostolic and the post-apostolic churches.

[27] The *second* Christian generation sees the activity and the person of the apostle as one and the same and identifies him with a permanent part of the building. 1 Tim. 3. 15 shows how this development was continued by the *third* Christian generation. Here the *church* is the "pillar and bulwark (*hedraiōma*) of the truth". Our discussion shows that statements of this kind are always linked to the foundation, which is Jesus Christ, and must not be taken in an absolute sense. The church is the bulwark of the truth only in so far as it is constituted by this truth (Jesus Christ) which has been entrusted to it as the apostolic *parathēkē* which it has to preserve.

[28] J. Gnilka, *Epheserbrief*, p. 156.

image. In the same verse Jesus Christ is described as the "corner-stone" of this foundation.[29] But the corner-stone gives form to the foundation, so that Jesus Christ is also the norm for the apostles and prophets—the form of the foundation is that of Christ. The form of Christ, given to the foundation by the corner-stone, is also imparted to what is built upon the foundation, since the corner-stone links the foundation with the building.[30] It gives its shape both to the foundation and to the building, and unites the foundation and the walls which lie on it. That is, Jesus Christ is the norm both for the apostles and prophets and for the Church that follows. He unites both the apostolic and the post-apostolic Church, since it is in him and through him that the whole structure is joined together (Eph. 2. 21). The norm is Jesus Christ, who, in his human life and his death, brought peace between Jews and Gentiles and reconciled both to God (cf. Eph. 2. 14–17).[31] The apostles and prophets are *norma normans* for the Church only in so far as they are *norma normata* by Jesus Christ and the gospel.

2. *The Growing Building*

The building of the Church which rises on this foundation is not, however, complete. It has still to "grow" into a holy temple, which is holy not of itself, but only "in the Lord". The static image of foundation and corner-stone turns into the dynamic image of *growth*. The mention of "growth" intro-

---

[29] J. Jeremias, in "Gōnia", etc., in *Theologisches Wörterbuch*, I, 792 f., and "Lithos", in *Theologisches Wörterbuch*, IV, 272–83, has sought to prove that the *akrogōnaios* is not the corner-stone of a building, but the keystone which tops the building. Cf. the well-supported criticism of this thesis in E. Percy, *Die Probleme der Kolosser- und Epheserbriefe* (Lund, 1946), pp. 329–32, 485–8; F. Mussner, *Christus das All und die Kirche*, pp. 108 f.; J. Pfammatter, *op. cit.*, pp. 143–51. Likewise the head in the similar image of the Church as the body of Christ (Eph. 4. 15 f.) is not placed upon the body as the conclusion of its growth, but co-ordinates (*synharmologoumenon*) the growing body. The Church is always determined by Christ, not merely as its goal, but from the very first as its *archē*.

[30] F. Mussner, *Christus das All und die Kirche*, p. 109.

[31] For the interpretation cf. F. Mussner, *Christus das All und die Kirche*, pp. 79–104; J. Gnilka, "Christus unser Friede—ein Friedenser-löserlied in Eph. 2. 14–17", in *Die Zeit Jesu* (*Festschrift* for H. Schlier, Freiburg, 1970), pp. 190–207.

duces into the non-organic image of "building" an element of the organic image of the Church as the "body of Christ" (cf. Eph. 4. 11–16) which is also understood as growing and as built (Eph. 4. 12, 15 f.). Even the "body of Christ" had not yet grown up in all its members to "mature manhood" and to "the measure of the stature of the fullness of Christ" (Eph. 4. 13). Different ministries have as their purpose the "building up" and growth of that body (Eph. 4. 11 f.). The exhortation to Christians to grow by speaking the truth in love (Eph. 4. 15) shows that the growth of love is not an automatic process, but a constant task. The aim of this growth is Christ (Eph. 4. 15), or the full identity of the body with him as a "grown man" (Eph. 4. 13). But this aim is not merely something for the future, for as the head of the body Christ is already co-ordinating the growth of the body (Eph. 4. 16), just as, as the corner-stone, he joined together the whole building. In spite of its permanent foundation and corner-stone the Church is never perfect. "It is . . . always the Church becoming, and never the Church at its goal."[32] It is always provisional, a house still being built, but never the completed house of glory.

III. Conclusions

The images taken from the language of building in the two passages are not exactly parallel, because of the different points of view of the apostolic and post-apostolic Church, but they have a great deal in common. Paul sees his preaching of the gospel of Jesus Christ as founding and constituting the Church. From the post-apostolic point of view of the Epistle to the Ephesians, the generation of the early Church and apostolic and prophetic teachers, is understood as the foundation on which the Church is based, and as the beginning of the overflowing of the eschatological salvation present in Jesus into the universal Church of Jews and Gentiles. The apostolic Church is of permanent importance as in fact the *archē* of the universal Church, but it is not the norm for the post-apostolic Church in isolation from the eschatological event of Christ. Even the apostle remains bound by the unchangeable gospel; even the form of the

[32] J. Gnilka, *Epheserbrief*, p. 159.

foundation of the apostles and prophets is determined by the corner-stone. God's eschatological gift of salvation in Jesus Christ, proclaimed in the apostolic kerygma, is the event which constitutes the Church, the base which supports it and the norm which always determines its form.

Because the Church is the eschatological community not in itself, but only in and through its relationship with the *eschaton,* Jesus Christ, it can be called the temple of God, but must never be understood as a building already complete. This building is still growing and is never complete within time. But growth means that a distinction can be made between what is fixed and what is changeable. What is fixed is the eschatological foundation of Jesus Christ and its universal spread through the apostolic Church. Thus the symbolism of building and temple ought not to be understood in purely static terms, but must be recognized as a unity of static and dynamic elements. This excludes any form of ecclesiastical triumphalism, even the anxious, romantic and reactionary triumphalism which can understand the present changes in the Church only as a breaking down of the building of the Church from a former state of perfection. But because the building up upon the foundation must be tested by the judgment, there is no place for the naïve evolutionism which seeks to understand the growth of the building as progress from glory to glory. The Church is both a building and a building site.

Translated by R. A. Wilson

André Lemaire

From Services to Ministries: "Diakoniai" in the First Two Centuries

THE study of the services and ministries of the Church in the first two centuries faces two main difficulties.[1] On the one hand, it is always difficult for an historian to grasp a religious movement just as it comes into being, and on the other there is a strong temptation to go so far in using the present to reconstruct the past that we project our modern ideas on to the early Church. Only a precise and rigorous analysis of the written evidence we possess from this earliest period will allow us to avoid this trap. Since it is impossible to carry out this analysis in detail here, I shall, in this article, use previously published work in an attempt to distinguish the main lines of the evolution of services in the Church during the first two centuries.[2]

I. THE "PRIMITIVE" COMMUNITY IN JERUSALEM

We have no direct contemporary evidence from this period, but it is possible, provided we exercise care, to draw on the sources used by Luke in the first chapters of the Acts of the Apostles.[3]

The first service attested in the emerging Christian community

---

[1] The Greek word *diakonia* can be translated as either "service" or "ministry"; it refers to any function whether institutionalized ("ministry" suggests this) or not.

[2] See the present author's work, *Les ministères aux origines de l'Eglise* (Paris, 1971) and the bibliography on pp. 219–36.

[3] For Luke's evidence cf. R. Schnackenburg, "Lukas als Zeuge verschiedener Gemeindestrukturen", *Bibel und Leben* 12 (1971), pp. 232–47.

is that of "the Twelve". The expression belongs to the oldest stratum of the gospels, and the traditional description of Judas in the passion narratives as "one of the Twelve" is itself proof that the existence of this group goes back to the earthly ministry of Jesus. According to the source which reports the election of Matthias and was used by Luke in Acts 1. 15–26, being a member of the group of the Twelve means having a part in a service (*diakonia*, Acts 1. 17, 25) consisting of witnessing to the resurrection (Acts 1. 22) before the "house of Israel" (Acts 2. 36).

This function is restricted to a group of twelve men because it concerns the twelve tribes of Israel;[4] it is therefore fundamentally part of a Jewish context. The Twelve are the leaders of the new community; as well as bearing witness to the resurrection, that is, proclaiming the good news both to the Jewish crowds (Acts 2. 14–15; 3. 2) and to the disciples gathered in houses (Acts 5. 42), they are still responsible for the management of the community's funds (Acts 4. 34–5, 36–7; 5. 2).

According to the source underlying Acts 6. 1–6, the management of the relief fund was a cause of tensions between the two groups of Christian Jews who made up the new community: "the Hellenists murmured against the Hebrews because their widows were neglected in the daily distribution" (Acts 6. 2). Faced with an incident which could have led to serious trouble, the Twelve realized that it would be better to let the Hellenists set up an autonomous organization and take responsibility for their own needs. This group therefore chose "seven men of good repute, full of the Spirit and of wisdom" (Acts 6. 3), and the Twelve appointed them "to this duty". These seven, who are nothing to do with the deacons, were to be responsible, within the group of the Hellenists, not only for the daily relief of widows but also, and chiefly, for the proclamation of the word (Acts 6. 9–10).

This preaching soon provoked a violent reaction from the Jewish authorities. A persecution began, Stephen was stoned and the Hellenists dispersed (Acts 8. 1); from this time on the Seven no longer have any purpose, and disappear as a special group. One of them, Philip, turned into an itinerant preacher of the

[4] Cf. Mt. 19. 28; Lk. 22. 30; and A. Jaubert, "La symbolique des Douze", in *Hommages à A. Dupont-Sommer* (Paris, 1971), pp. 453–60.

good news (Acts 8) in Samaria and the Mediterranean coastal plain.

The Twelve are not mentioned again after the death of Stephen. Like the Seven, they seem to have quickly disappeared as a permanent group. When Herod "killed James the brother of John with the sword" (Acts 12. 2) there is no longer any mention of the choice of a replacement to make up the number of the Twelve. There are two possible reasons for this disintegration of the Twelve as a group. First, persecution led to the dispersal of the members of the group (cf. Acts 12. 19) and, in addition, the Twelve were a typically Jewish structure: from the moment when pagans too had access to baptism this structure began to break down and a new division of responsibilities took place. James remained in Jerusalem, while Peter became a more or less itinerant missionary.

The two groups, the Twelve and the Seven, are thus characteristic of the primitive Jerusalem community. They were soon broken up by the quickly changing historical situation, and it is typical that Paul, while he knows "James, Cephas and John" (Gal. 2. 9), never uses the expression "the Twelve" except in 1 Cor. 15. 4, where he quotes a traditional confession of faith which probably comes from the primitive Jerusalem community.

II. The "Apostolic" Age

This period ends with the deaths of the great apostles Peter and Paul around the years 64–67. The most reliable evidence from this period is the collection of the genuine letters of Paul.[5] To these epistles can be added certain written sources used in Acts, and most of the *Didache*.[6]

The work of the Twelve was directed towards the conversion and government of the twelve tribes of Israel. The Spirit soon revealed, however, that the pagans were also called to be members of the people of God,[7] and the consequent need to adapt the

[5] For studies of the ministries in Paul's thought, see the articles by R. Pesch, P. Grelot and J. Budillon in *Istina* (1971), pp. 437–88.

[6] On the date of the *Didache* see A. Lemaire, *Les ministères aux origines de l'Eglise*, pp. 140, 189.

[7] See M. Hengel, "Die Ursprünge der christlichen Mission", *New Testament Studies* 18 (1971), pp. 15–38.

structures of the Church to the new situation created the apostles'
missionary role.[8] Thus Peter and John are sent as official envoys
from Jerusalem to the Samaritans (Acts 8. 14 ff.), and Barnabas
is sent to Antioch (Acts 11. 22). It was in this city that the disciples first received the name Christians, and there also that the
mission to the diaspora and the Greeks was organized (Acts 11.
19–20).

The source used in Acts 13. 1 gives us some details of the
division of responsibilities in the Antiochian community: "Now
in the church at Antioch there were prophets and teachers, Barnabas, Symeon who was called Niger, Lucius of Cyrene, Manaen,
a member of the court of Herod the tetrarch, and Saul." The
members of this group are all Hellenists; they come from the
Jewish diaspora. Barnabas, the Levite from Cyprus, had already
distinguished himself in Jerusalem, where he seems to have been
regarded as a prophet (Acts 4. 36). Saul too had lived for some
time in Jerusalem, where, "at the feet of Gamaliel" (Acts 22. 3),
he had received a rabbinic education, so that it is hardly surprising to find him teaching with Barnabas "for a whole year" (Acts
11. 26).

In Acts 13. 2 these "prophets and teachers" are described as
"conducting the worship of the Lord (*leitourgountōn tō Kyriō*)
and fasting", and it was in the course of such "liturgical" activity
that the Holy Spirit revealed himself in an oracle: "Set apart for
me Barnabas and Saul for the work to which I have called them."
This is a "prophetic" oracle,[9] similar to that of the prophet
Agabus, which opens with the formula, "Thus says the Holy
Spirit" (Acts 21. 10–11).[10] As their name indicates, the "prophets
and teachers" of Antioch were responsible for the regular teaching and the proclamation of the inspired word in the liturgical
assemblies.

But what was the new work to which Barnabas and Saul were
called? "Being sent off by the Holy Spirit", they made their way

---

[8] For the distinction between the titles "Twelve" and "Apostles" see
J. Dupont, "Le nom d'Apôtres a-t-il été donné aux Douze par Jésus?",
Orient Chrétien (1965), pp. 445 ff.; A. Lemaire, *Les ministères*, p. 195.

[9] On Christian prophets see E. Cothenet, "Le Prophétisme dans le
N.T.", in *Suppl. Dict. Bib.* VIII (Paris, 1971), cols. 1222–1337; "Prophétisme et ministère d'après le N.T.", *La Maison-Dieu* 107 (1971), pp. 29–50.

[10] Cf. also the oracles to the seven churches in Rev. 3.

through Cyprus, Pamphilia, Pisidia and Lycaonia, preaching the good news of Jesus' resurrection in the synagogues, before finally giving an account of the "work" they had done to the community in Antioch (Acts 14. 26–27). More precisely, in Acts 14. 4, 14, where Luke follows literally the source he is using, Barnabas and Saul are called "apostles". Antioch thus appears as the missionary centre from which apostles spread out over the whole of the diaspora, and it is characteristic that it should be in an Antiochian source that we meet for the first time the technical term "apostle", meaning an official representative of both the Holy Spirit and the community or, better, of the community acting under the power of the Holy Spirit, sent to spread the good news.

Paul, whose first mission has just been described, has gone down in the history of the Church as the type of the "apostle".[11] He describes his mission very clearly in his letters: "Christ did not send me to baptize, but to preach the gospel. . . . Woe to me if I do not preach the gospel!" (1 Cor. 1. 17; 9. 16). He insists on his right to the title of apostle: "an apostle not from man, but through Jesus Christ and God the Father, who raised him from the dead" (Gal. 1. 1). This language, however, born of polemic climate,[12] should not make us forget the human roots of Paul's apostolate. Paul knows that he is not the only apostle, admits that others were apostles before him (Gal. 1. 17) and refers several times to his admission to the apostolate together with Barnabas.[13] Even more, he himself recalls the limits of his mission by mentioning the "Jerusalem agreement": "and when they perceived the grace that was given to me, James and Cephas and John, who were reputed to be pillars, gave to me and Barnabas the right hand of fellowship, that we should go to the Gentiles and they to the circumcised" (Gal. 2. 9). This very important agreement reveals an organization of apostolic work embracing the whole of the Mediterranean world. As in the past, when the Seven were appointed, the division of areas is not geographical,

[11] See K. Kertelge, "Das Apostelamt des Paulus. Sein Ursprung und seine Bedeutung", *Biblische Zeitschrift* 14 (1970), pp. 161–81.

[12] See C. K. Barrett, "Paul's Opponents in II Corinthians", *New Testament Studies* 17 (1971), pp. 233–54.

[13] 1 Cor. 9. 6; Gal. 2. 1, 9; see E. E. Ellis, "Paul and his Co-Workers", *New Testament Studies* 17 (1971), pp. 437–52.

but rather "ethnocultural", Jews on the one side, pagans on the other, with a number of apostles responsible for the apostolate to either group.[14]

It is therefore normal for Paul to place the apostolate first among the manifestations of the Spirit in the Church. Referring to the diversity of members in the body of Christ, he declares: "God has appointed in the church first apostles, second prophets, third teachers" (1 Cor. 12. 28). Paul is here quoting a traditional list, which probably comes from the Antiochian community.[15] We can say more about the formula Paul uses.

These three forms of service of the word are given an official, institutional character by the use of the verb *etheto*, "he has placed, he has appointed" and by the careful ordering: first, second, third.

These services are included in a list of "gifts" (*charismata*). Paul therefore makes no contrast between "institutional" and "charismatic" functions;[16] in his view, everyone ought to use the gifts he has received for the service of others, and he places gifts (*charismata*) in parallel with services (*diakoniai*, 1 Cor. 12. 4–5).

These three groups have no monopoly of gifts: "then workers of miracles, then healers". All Paul says is that, for the task of "building up the church", some gifts are more important than others (1 Cor. 12. 28; 14. 1, 12, 26).

Paul's description of the pre-eminent role of apostles, prophets and teachers is in complete agreement with the evidence of the *Didache*, the Christian missionary manual of the second half of the first century which was probably produced in Antioch.

In the *Didache* the apostle is an itinerant, and there is thus an instruction that "every apostle who comes to you be received as the Lord" (xi. 4), just as Paul was received by the Galatians (Gal. 4. 14). The prophet can be recognized because he speaks "in a spirit" (*en pneumati*) (*Did.* xi. 7, 8; cf. 1 Cor. 14. 29–32), and he proclaims the thanksgiving: "let the prophets give thanks

---

[14] Barnabas was recognized as an apostle with the same status as Paul, and there must have been others.

[15] Paul's missionary activity is linked with the Antioch community; see Acts 13. 1–2; 14. 26; 15. 35–36; 18. 22; Gal. 2. 11.

[16] See A. Rodenas, "Teologia biblica de los carismas", *Estudios biblicos* 30 (1971), pp. 345–60.

(*eucharistein*) as much as they wish" (*Did*. x. 7; cf. 1 Cor. 14. 15–17). In addition, he may teach (*Did*. xi. 10), and he is often associated with the teacher (*Did*. xiii. 2), and we find the general description "the official service (*leitourgian*) of the prophets and teachers" (*Did*. xv. 1).

These apostles, prophets and teachers carry out a specialized service which is real "work", and therefore the community has an obligation to meet their material needs. The itinerant apostle is entitled to hospitality in the communities he visits (*Did*. xi. 4), and Paul insists that he has a right to "food and drink" and "to be accompanied by a Christian woman, like the other apostles", "to refrain from working for a living" (1 Cor. 9. 4–6) and to be supported by the community (1 Thess. 2. 7). The *Didache* says that the prophet who takes up residence in a community is "worth his keep" and says specifically that he is to be given the first fruits of the produce (*Did*. xiii.). It justifies the same right in the case of the teacher by the principle, "the worker is worthy of his food",[17] and Paul is probably referring to this maxim in 1 Cor. 9. 14.

We see then that the Antiochian source of Acts, the letters of Paul and the recommendations of the *Didache* agree in their description of a fairly precise organization of the various services of the word attached to the missionary centre at Antioch between A.D. 40 and 70. The vigour of this Hellenistic community should not, however, make us forget the other local communities where the organization of services may have been different.

In Jerusalem, James and the presbyters were the leaders of a Jewish Christian community. The institution of the presbyters is not reported by the author of Acts; it is taken for granted—any Palestinian Jewish community was organized on the "presbyteral" model and had a college of elders at its head. According to Acts 15 and 21. 18 ff., the presbyters gathered around James saw to it that the life of the Christians was in accord with the word of God contained in the Scriptures which had been fulfilled in Jesus; they also managed the relief fund and in that capacity received the gifts sent by the other communities (Acts 11. 29–30; cf. Gal. 2. 10). It is likely that presbyters were appointed on this

[17] *Did*. xiii. 2; see Mt. 10. 10; Lk. 10. 7; 1 Tim. 5. 18.

model in the new Jewish Christian communities in the diaspora and that it was Jewish Christian apostles, perhaps Jude and Silas (Acts 15. 22 ff.),[18] who "appointed elders ... in every church" in Cilicia and Southern Asia Minor (Acts 14. 23).

Paul's letters several times mention services within the local communities. As early as the First Epistle to the Thessalonians, Paul asks for consideration for those who carry out this work. The verbs used in 1 Thess. 5. 12–13 refer to the function of presiding and the service of the word; Paul asks for particular attention to the latter: "Do not quench the Spirit, do not despise prophecy" (1 Thess. 5. 19–20). The prophetic service still comes first among the community services in Corinth (cf. 1 Cor. 14). Paul also mentions the gifts of miracle-working, healing, helping, administration and speaking in tongues (1 Cor. 12. 28–30), but he does not seem to connect them with any definite service of the church; this seems to have been organized, at least in part, by Stephanas and his household, who "have devoted themselves to the service (*diakonia*) of the saints" (1 Cor. 16. 15).

Paul does not know the Roman community personally and therefore makes only a few general references to the organization of community services there (Rom. 12. 6–8). In contrast, in Rom. 16, probably originally a note addressed to the church of Ephesus, he takes the trouble to mention by name those who are or have been engaged in the service of the church, for example: "Phoebe, a servant of the church at Cenchreae" (Rom. 16. 1), Prisca and Aquila, who let the assembly meet in their house, and many others whose devotion to the service of the gospel Paul has experienced. Writing to the Galatians, Paul makes no more than a brief reference to "him who teaches the word" and asks that his material needs should be seen to (Gal. 6. 6). He is more emphatic about the service Epaphras has given to the community at Colossae (Col. 1. 7; 4. 12–13); Epaphras remained with Paul, and in his place Archippus received, in the Lord, responsibility for the service (Col. 4. 17).

In the community at Philippi this function seems to have been carried out by a definite group whom Paul, at the beginning of his letter, describes as "overseers and ministers" (*episkopoi kai*

[18] See Lemaire, *op. cit.*, pp. 66–7.

diakonoi). There has been much discussion about their precise role, and our only additional information comes from the *Didache*: "Appoint *episkopous* and *diakonous* worthy of the Lord, men who are gentle and not avaricious, but truthful and of proven worth; for they too fill the office of prophets and teachers for you" (*Did.* xv. 1). From this it seems that these overseers and ministers, who came from the community, were responsible, like the prophets and teachers, for the service of preaching and the proclamation of thanksgiving.

Each local community tended to form its own organization and take more or less responsibility for its own needs. In the Jewish Christian communities these services were organized on the traditional "presbyteral" model, while the mission to the Gentiles tried to respect the cultural distinctiveness of the new communities; as a description of those who organized the services, instead of the word "presbyter", the vaguer and more general term "overseers and ministers" was preferred.

III. The Age of the "Evangelists and Pastors"[19]

"It is impossible to list the names of all those who then, at the time of the first succession to the apostles, became pastors or evangelists in the churches of the world."[20] This remark by Eusebius of Caesarea shows very well how from now on the Church was implanted more or less everywhere in the Mediterranean basin and how the emphasis was increasingly placed on pastoral service in the local churches. This is the period of the final editing of the Epistle to the Ephesians, of the composition of the gospels and the Acts of the Apostles, of the Epistle to the Hebrews, 1 Peter and the pastoral epistles.

The author of the Epistle to the Hebrews makes only a few very brief references to the service of the community: "Obey your leaders and submit to them; for they are keeping watch over your souls, as men who will have to give account" (Heb. 13. 17). The responsibilities of these "leaders" thus appear to be mainly pastoral.[21]

[19] Eph. 4. 11; see Lemaire, *op. cit.*, pp. 106–7.
[20] Eusebius, *Hist. Eccles.* III. xxxvii. 4.
[21] The title *hēgoumenos* (leader) is peculiar to this epistle and probably reflects the usage of the Roman community.

In the address to the presbyters of Ephesus, community service is presented explicitly in a pastoral image: "Take heed to yourselves and to all the flock, in which the Holy Spirit has made you guardians (*episkopous*), to feed the church of God" (Acts 20. 28). The same is true of the advice to the presbyters in 1 Pet. 5. 2–4:[22] "Tend the flock of God that is your charge, exercising the oversight not by constraint but willingly, as God would have you, not for shameful gain but eagerly, not as domineering over those in your charge but being examples to the flock." The association of presbyters and pastors recurs in the Christian fragment of the *Ascension of Isaiah*:[23] "In those days there will be many who love offices though they lack wisdom, and there will be many unjust presbyters and pastors who oppress their flocks, and they will tear them apart because they have not holy pastors.... Among them there will be great hatred among pastors and presbyters for each other."[24] This passage is similar to the prophecy of the coming of "fierce wolves ... not sparing the flock" in Acts 20. 29. These three texts show that one of the main problems of this period was the unworthy behaviour of pastors: they tended to dominate and oppress their flock, while quarrelling among themselves; the jealousy of pastors was already beginning to split the Church.

It was in this context that the pastoral epistles were produced.[25] The author offers them as a remedy for this lamentable situation, by insisting on the qualities required in candidates for the ministry and for the rules to be followed in dealing with established presbyteries.[26] He makes Paul say to Titus, "This is why I left you in Crete, that you might amend what was defective and appoint elders in every town" (Tit. 1. 5). While the term *epis-*

---

[22] See J. H. Elliott, "Ministry and Church Order ...", *Catholic Biblical Quarterly* 32 (1970), pp. 367–91.

[23] This fragment is dated "between 88 and 100" by E. Tisserant, *Ascension de Isaïe* (Paris, 1909), p. 60.

[24] *Ascension of Isaiah*, III. 23–24, 29, 113, 115.

[25] See A. Lemaire, "Epîtres pastorales: redaction et théologie", *Bulletin de Théologie biblique* (1972), pp. 24–41.

[26] See N. Brox, "Historische und theologische Probleme der Pastoralbriefe des N.T. Zur Dokumentation der frühchristlichen Amtsgeschichte", *Kairos* 11 (1960), pp. 81–94.

kopos is used twice, it can be applied to any "presbyter",[27] and the author insists on the value of "presbyteral" ordination by the laying on of hands of which Timothy's is the paradigm (1 Tim. 4. 14; 2 Tim. 1. 6). It is wrong, however, to lay hands on anyone (1 Tim. 5. 22), because the church has already suffered too much from unworthy pastors, "drunkards, violent, lovers of money" (cf. 1 Tim. 3. 3). Among the qualities required of the candidate, two seem particularly characteristic: first, he must be "an apt teacher" (1 Tim. 3. 2), and "hold firm to the true word as taught" (Tit. 1. 9), and in addition must be a good husband and father and "manage his own household well, keeping his children submissive and respectful in every way" (1 Tim. 3. 4).

These qualities should enable candidates to carry out their ministry for the greatest good of all: "Let the elders who rule well be considered worthy of double honour, especially those who labour in preaching and teaching." This statement comes at the beginning of a paragraph which could be called "the law of the presbyter" (1 Tim. 5. 17–20). Those who perform their double task of presiding and teaching well merit both honour and reward from the community, but those who are unworthy are to be rebuked "in the presence of all"; but in the latter case it is necessary to act with the greatest prudence and "never admit any charge against an elder except on the evidence of two or three witnesses".

It is not certain that there were deacons in all the churches;[28] there were in Ephesus, but there is no mention of any in Crete. According to 1 Tim. 3. 8–13, their work can be carried out equally well by women as by men, and their duties are very close to those of presbyters. A few differences in the qualities required, the absence of hospitality and the insistence on "confidence" (*parrhēsia*), probably mean that these deacons are itinerant ministers doing the same work as the old members of missionary teams. The time of the great missions is over and these ministers go out from a centre which has an "evangelist" like Timothy at Ephesus (2 Tim. 4. 5) or Philip at Caesarea (Acts 21. 8).

[27] See P. Burke, "The Monarchical Episcopate at the End of the First Century", *Journal of Ecumenical Studies* 7 (1970), pp. 499–518.

[28] See E. P. Echlin, "The Origins of the Permanent Deacon", *American Ecclesiastical Review* 2 (1970), pp. 92–105.

In this way, after the death of the apostles, the Church re-organized itself to give increasing attention to the problems of the local communities. Faced with new dangers threatening it from within, unorthodox teaching, rivalry between presbyters, abuses of power by pastors, the Church fixed its doctrinal and disciplinary traditions in a more precise form. This drive for unification and codification resulted in the generalization of the "presbyteral" model inherited from Jewish tradition.

IV. The Age of the "Apostolic Fathers"

Our evidence for the organization of Church functions at the end of the first century and in the first half of the second is contained in four important texts or groups of texts. Two come from Rome, the letter of Clement of Rome to the Corinthians and the Shepherd of Hermas, and the two others come from Asia Minor, the letters of Ignatius of Antioch and Polycarp of Smyrna.

A disciplinary problem had made the church of Rome write to the church of Corinth. The church of Corinth had just re-belled against its presbyters (xlvii. 6), and Rome judged the rebellion unacceptable: "We consider... that it is not just to remove from their ministry (*leitourgia*) those who were appointed by (the apostles), or later on by other eminent men, with the consent of the whole church. ... Nor will it be a small sin on our part if we drive from their office (*episkopē*) those who have offered the gifts with blameless piety" (xliv. 3, 4).

The presbyters, who are sometimes also called "leaders" as in the Epistle to the Hebrews, thus seem to be appointed for life. Their office is essentially pastoral, and there is now hardly any mention of the service of the word, while precise references to cultic functions appear, as in "offer the gifts" (1 Clem. xliv. 3). The institutional character of this structure is emphasized by Clement himself, with his references to "established presbyters" (1 Clem. liv. 2) to whom the dissidents must submit (lvii. 1).

It is more difficult to use the evidence of the Shepherd of Hermas because of the literary form and composite character of this work. For the most part it confirms the evidence of 1 Clement: the presbyters are at the head of the Church (*prohē-goumenoi*) and preside over it (Vis. II. iv. 3) by taking the principal seats in the assemblies (Vis. III. ix. 7), and there is hardly any reference to their exercising a ministry of the word. This ministry seems above all the work of the "prophets", of whom Hermas is the type (Mand. XII. iii. 3): "The prophetic angel who is with him fills that man and, filled with the Holy Spirit, he speaks to the people as the Lord wishes" (Mand. XI. 9). It seems that presbyters and prophets share the duties of the ministry, the presbyters exercising authority and the prophets the service of the word, but only in submission to the presbyters (Vis. III. i. 8; Mand. XI. viii. 12).

The letters of Ignatius of Antioch reveal a very detailed organization of ministries. Each local church is governed by a leader, the "bishop". "No one is to do any church business without the bishop. The only eucharist which should be regarded as valid is one which the bishop, or someone appointed by him, presides. . . . Anyone who acts without the bishop's knowledge serves the devil" (Smyrn. viii. 1; ix. 1). It is hard not to call this organization a monarchy! Nevertheless the bishop does not exercise this role alone; he is surrounded by a council, the presbyterium (Smyrn. viii. 1; xii. 2). The presbytery must be in harmony with the bishop like the strings on a harp (Ignatius, Eph. iv. 1), for it is fitting that Christians should be united in submission to the bishop and the presbyterium (Eph. ii. 2). The unusual force of this insistence on the authority of the bishop and the presbyterium makes the contrast all the sharper with the almost complete absence of any reference to a teaching function. Ignatius does say that the bishops are "in the mind (*gnōmē*) of Jesus Christ" (Eph. iii. 2), but even when he writes to Polycarp he stresses his duties as a pastor and makes no reference to his role as teacher. It is indeed typical that he should justify the silence of a bishop: "he could do more by silence than those who are full of empty talk" (Phil. i. 1).

This makes it all the more interesting that Ignatius, in recalling the importance of deacons (Trall. ii. 3), should mention their participation in the ministry of the "word of God",[29] at the same

[29] See Ignatius, Phil. xi. 1: ". . . Philo, the deacon from Cicilia, a man of good reputation, who is now serving me in the word of God (*en logō theou*)."

time as their suitability to be sent on missions which involved travel.

The epistle of Polycarp, apart from a few points of language,[30] confirms this picture of the organization of church offices in Asia Minor at the beginning of the second century. Writing on the occasion of the deposition of the "presbyter" Valens (xi), Polycarp approves this action, and if we are to judge from Polycarp's vehement denunciation of avarice, Valens and his wife had been guilty of misusing funds. Polycarp takes the opportunity to urge the presbyters to give proof of their zeal and kindness in their pastoral duties (vi), but makes no reference to the service of the word.

The Apostolic Fathers thus bear witness to an increasingly fixed structure of the ministries; the presbyteral model is now ·universal, but has been developed by an increase in the power of one of the members, who becomes the leader and the representative of the community, the bishop, while the other ministers, prophets or deacons, play a less and less prominent role. This increase in uniformity was accompanied by a greater emphasis on pastoral authority at the expense of the service of the word.

A striking impression at the end of this study is the diversity in the organization of church functions in different communities and periods. Without claiming to trace a homogeneous evolution, we can say that the organizational form which was at first very flexible and adapted itself to the new needs of the Church and the inspirations of the Spirit became more and more fixed, institutionalized and uniform.

There are probably two main causes for this development. First, the disappearance of the first "witnesses" brought serious dangers of error and deviation; it was necessary to ensure the uniformity of teaching, and for this purpose the Church adopted the model of rabbinic ordination for presbyters as a symbol and guarantee of fidelity in the transmission of the "deposit". Secondly, as the communities became more and more numerous and scattered, unity was no longer automatic; in order to preserve it the Church adopted a more and more structured organization and increased the power of the bishop, the leader of the local

---

[30] Polycarp does not use the term *episkopos*. It is likely that he took the office for granted, but prefers to use the traditional title "presbyter".

community, whose responsibility it became to watch over its internal unity and its communion with the other churches.

At the same time as this gradual development of a structure a change can be seen taking place in the balance of tasks in the ministries. During the first two phases the service of the word has an unchallengeable priority (cf. Acts 6. 4; 1 Cor. 1. 17); during the third stage the emphasis is as much on the pastoral role as on teaching,[31] and finally, in the period of the Apostolic Fathers, it is clear that the teaching function has slipped into the background while pastoral authority is heavily emphasized. This development can be explained in part by the success of the mission and the needs of the newly established communities, but it is likely that it should be seen as the result of the increasingly serious doubts cast on the teaching function by the deviations of some teachers.

What conclusions can we draw from this historical study? What can we learn today from the organization of church functions in the first two centuries? It is wise not to try to give too quick an answer to these two questions. History never provides ready-made solutions; it only enables us to step back and see more clearly what is essential and what depends on circumstances. Taking advantage of this facility, we find that the service of the word and the service of unity seem to be essential to the life of the Church, but the forms and structures of these services are adaptable and can be changed as required.

Translated by Francis McDonagh

---

[31] Note the expression "evangelists and pastors" (Eph. 4. 11), which is characteristic of this period, and the double function of governing and teaching attributed to the presbyters in 1 Tim. 5. 17.

Peter Kearney

New Testament Incentives for a Different Ecclesial Order?

THE FACT that the New Testament reveals a variety of church orders has become a commonplace. It is helpful to note this fact at the outset, for it gives rise at once to the question of possibilities for an order different from the one that the Catholic Church knows today. However, the mere fact of such difference is not sufficient to answer the question in the title of this study. We must find what such a variety meant within the New Testament itself. Further, the New Testament canon was formed precisely because it was seen that not every age of the Church would be like the apostolic period; therefore, the picture which emerges from the earliest church orders cannot serve as a mirror image for the ideal of our own day. We must search further for the meaning of such variety for today. "Meaning" is a matter of expressing relationships; our whole effort will be an attempt to keep relationships in balance.

I. NEW TESTAMENT AWARENESS OF VARIETY IN CHURCH ORDER

How can these varieties be related to the intentions of Jesus himself? It has been argued that the foundation of the Church must be regarded as the work of Peter after his vision of the risen Christ rather than an outcome intended by the earthly Jesus.[1] Such a theory presupposes a discontinuity between the historical Jesus and the risen Christ not in harmony with the

[1] H. Conzelmann, "On the Analysis of the Confessional Formula in 1 Corinthians 15. 3–5", *Interpretation* 20 (1966), p. 22.

Catholic tradition of the Incarnation, but it does caution against carelessness in phrasing questions and seeking ready-made answers. If we ask quite simply "Did Jesus intend to found a Church with ministerial structures?", we probably have to answer "No", but the question itself is misleading in that it ignores the broader problem of the Church as a legitimate development of the ministry of Jesus. His preaching made available to man the gift of God's reign even before its perfect realization. This uniting of accomplishment with further anticipation was undoubtedly expressed in the Last Supper of Jesus as he looked forward to the heavenly banquet now anticipated in this farewell meal with his disciples (Luke 22. 16, 18). An imperfect realization of God's reign continued as the situation even after the resurrection of Jesus and is both the foundation for the re-enactment of the Last Supper (whether Jesus actually spoke the mandate to repeat the meal or not) and the legitimation of the ministries which grew up in that community who sought to serve the consuming interest of Jesus' life. Further, the establishment of these ministries can probably be related even more directly to the example of Jesus, who, even while preaching a message open to all men who would hear him, chose special groups for a particular share in his work, such as the intimate group Peter, James and John, and the circle of the Twelve, and gave to his disciples, even in his own lifetime, a share in his preaching mission. But even if the historical value of these data be questioned, there remains the ministry of Jesus himself, which is the ultimate foundation of the Church, as it seeks the perfection of what Jesus left incomplete.

The intentions of Jesus did not express a particular form of church order; this fact itself allows for the various types that arose. Besides, there is evidence that change was *consciously* recognized and accepted and did not occur simply at random. Thus the pre-Lucan tradition of Acts 13. 1–3 shows us that the Apostle Paul formed part of a council of prophets and teachers at Antioch; we may no doubt see here a relationship to the pre-eminence of apostles, prophets and teachers in 1 Corinthians 12. 28. This same verse indicates a variety of other ministries at Corinth which have not yet given rise to personal titles (cf. also 1 Cor. 16. 15–16).

Rom. 12. 6–8 further discloses the non-systematic nature of Paul's thought on church structures, whether he is writing out of familiarity with the situation in Rome, or, as seems more likely, is expressing his experience with the churches he knows first-hand. Here the titles prophet and teacher are not side-by-side as in 1 Cor. and the charism of leadership can conceivably be exercised by one who belongs to neither group. At Philippi, Paul acknowledges the bishops and deacons (Phil. 1. 1), a grouping which perhaps arose on the initiative of the local church itself, since these titles appear in no other genuine Pauline epistle.[2] In addition, since James enjoyed a certain prominence at Jerusalem during one of Paul's visits there (Gal. 2. 9), it is possible that Paul had personal experience of the presbyteral structure which functioned there under the aegis of James. In view of Paul's strong desire to foster union between Jerusalem and his own mission field (Gal. 2. 2, 10; 1 Cor. 16. 1–4), it is striking that none of Paul's epistles gives evidence of an attempt to structure his churches on the model of Jerusalem (Acts 14. 23 forbids a categorical denial that Paul used such a model[3]).

Apart from Paul's own efforts, we find consciousness of change and development elsewhere. The three "pillars", James, Peter and John, probably express a new development in the Jerusalem church which Paul had not encountered at an earlier visit there (compare Gal. 1. 18–19; 2. 1, 9). The pre-eminence of these three was to be maintained into the post-apostolic period as their names became associated with encyclical letters of the New Testament, documents closely linked with Jewish Christianity (cf. James 1. 1, 1 Peter 1. 1; Apocalypse 1. 4). Among these letters, 1 Peter holds a special interest because of its attempt to bring Pauline theology into a Jewish-Christian system associated with Peter and the presbyteral structure (cf. 1 Pet. 5. 1–5).[4]

Luke also appears conscious of changing church structure as he marks out the developing stages under the Twelve (Acts 2. 42),

[2] J. Gnilka, "Geistliches Amt und Gemeinde nach Paulus", *Kairos* 11 (1969), 101, 103.
[3] M. Bourke, "Reflections on Church Order in the New Testament", *Cath. Bib. Quart.* 30 (1968), 502.
[4] W. Trilling, "Zum Petrusamt im Neuen Testament", *Theol. Quartal.* 151 (1971), 125–6.

then the (twelve) apostles[5] and presbyters (Acts 15), until the transition is made to the presbyters alone as Paul nears his death (Acts 20. 17–38). Luke has not developed an explicit theology of apostolic succession, but it is present in rudimentary form.

The Epistle to the Ephesians is noteworthy for stressing the theme of the developing Church, especially by modifying the Pauline image "Body of Christ" from an expression of unity into a symbol of growth as well (compare 1 Cor. 12. 12 and Eph. 4. 11–13). The offices listed in Eph 4. 11 allude to the enumeration in 1 Cor. 12. 28 and Rom. 12. 6–8, but Ephesians has some changes, notably the office of "pastor", which is not mentioned by Paul. The author of Ephesians is probably also conscious that the apostles and prophets belong to a generation that is past (Eph. 2. 20)[6] and that growth has therefore demanded a change in church structure.

The Gospel of Matthew has remarkably little explicit mention of church structures, but we can be certain that the Christian scribe was an important figure in that community (Mt. 13. 52); in giving this scribe a place in the tradition, Matthew was no doubt aware that more primitive structures had now undergone development, as he modified the older dyad "prophets and wise men" by the addition of "scribes" (Mt. 23. 34; a different adaptation has been made in Luke 11. 49).[7]

The author of the Pastoral Epistles was likewise aware of adding new elements to the church order tradition. The addressing of these letters to Timothy and Titus is best regarded as an artificial situation, in which these companions of Paul are composite figures of the ordaining "apostolic delegate" and the "presbyter-bishops" to be ordained.[8] The author must have been aware that in assigning to Timothy and Titus the role of organizing the local

[5] A. Lemaire, Les Ministères aux Origines de l'Eglise (Lectio Divina 68) (Paris, 1971), 183, holds that these apostles were actually the emissaries from Antioch to Jerusalem (Acts 15. 23). If so, it is none the less clear that Luke interprets them as the Twelve (15. 2).

[6] For an opposing view, cf. A. Satake, Die Gemeindeordnung in der Johannesapokalypse (Wissen. Monog. z. Alt. Test. 21) (Neukirchen–Vluyn, 1966), 6.

[7] Ibid., 180–5.

[8] N. Brox, "Historische und Theologische Probleme der Pastoralbriefe des Neuen Testaments", Kairos 11 (1969), 87–8, 90.

communities, he was going beyond any datum found in Acts or in the Pauline letters. It is also probable that he saw the roles of presbyter and bishop were being only gradually assimilated to each other in varying degrees in the different Pauline communities.[9] Thus his avoidance of any explicit reference to these offices in 2 Timothy and his general instruction that "trustworthy men" be appointed (2 Tim. 2. 2) can be understood as an attempt to cover the variety of local situations.

II. Conscious Striving for Unity and Uniformity

The preceding discussion remains one-sided unless balanced with the conscious development towards stabilized and uniform structure even within the New Testament period. The emergence of the presbyteral structure in the Pastoral Epistles is indicative of a trend in the later New Testament period. In these letters, structured office assumes special importance as the role of teacher, not necessarily linked to the governing function in the Pauline letters, now becomes the duty principally of the presbyter-bishop. The role of "evangelist" is now his also and he exercises it by guarding the deposit of faith (2 Tim. 4. 5), undoubtedly in a spirit quite different from that of the earlier evangelists, the charismatic preachers like Philip (Acts 21. 8). However, continuity with the past is maintained, for the mention of bishops and deacons in the same literary context (1 Tim. 3. 1–10) surely preserves their close association in Phil. 1. 1, where these two offices are mentioned together for the first time in any literature we possess.[10] By the time of Pastorals, the presbyteral office is being joined to the episcopal and the functions of both offices in Phil. 1. 1 are probably different in the later period,[11] but the attempt of these letters to achieve stability and uniformity by preserving continuity is unmistakable.

Analogous developments are found elsewhere in the New Testament. The presbyters around the heavenly throne in Apoc. 4. 4 may contain a hint of the order in the seven churches ad-

[9] H. von Campenhausen, *Ecclesiastical Authority and Spiritual Power* (Stanford, 1969), p. 107 (*Kirchliches Amt und geistliche Vollmacht*, Tübingen, 1953).
[10] J. Gnilka, *op. cit.*, 101.   [11] *Ibid.*, 103.

dressed at the beginning of this book. The possible citation of the "apostolic decree" in Apoc. 2. 14, 20 (cf. Acts 15. 29) suggests the possibility of Jerusalem influence even in the structure of the Apocalypse churches, as does the mention of presbyters in the church of Ephesus (Acts 20. 17), one of the same seven (Apoc. 2. 1). The matter is controverted, however, and some deny to these presbyters as well as to the "angels" of the churches any reference to visible church order.[12] A more secure analogy can be found in Acts 14. 23, the establishment of presbyteral colleges in the churches which Paul and Barnabas visited in retracing their steps back to Antioch. Because Paul has left us relatively little detail about the organization of his churches, one should hesitate to dismiss this notice as purely unhistorical, but it does appear parallel to the mandate of Paul to establish presbyter-bishops in the churches of the Pastorals. In both situations, the churches are in a transitional stage from a Pauline variety of forms towards a more structured uniform system influenced by the Jewish-Christian presbyteral model. There is a similar development in Ephesians, where the "pastor" (Eph. 4. 11) implies the "shepherding" role sometimes associated with the presbyteral office (Acts 20. 28; 1 Pet. 5. 1–4).

As previously noted, the spreading influence of Jewish-Christian structural models is shown by the importance given to the presbyteral office in 1 Peter, a letter addressed to an area approximately that of the Pauline mission and constructed in clear dependence on Pauline theology. It is noteworthy that elsewhere prominence is given to Peter in the interest of expressing the unity of the Church, but without implications for uniform church structure being drawn. The role of Peter as foundation rock of the universal Church (Matt. 16. 18) expresses well the Jewish-Christian interest of Matthew's gospel (cf. Gal. 2. 8 for the role of Peter in the Jewish-Christian mission). However, in his own post-apostolic period, Matthew gives us no indication of any special church structure which expresses the union of the Church in Peter. His function as keeper of the keys is continued by the

---

[12] Thus A. Satake, *op. cit.*, 149, 154, and E. Schweizer, *Church Order in the New Testament* Studies in Biblical Theology 32) (London, 1961), see Note 16, 13e (*Gemeinde und Gemeindeordnung im Neuen Testament*, Zürich, 1959).

Christian scribe (Matt. 13. 52; compare Isaiah 22. 15, 22; 36. 3)[13] and the power of binding and loosing endures in the activity of the local church (Matt. 18. 17–18),[14] a community whose structure remains in a studied obscurity (note the command to avoid honorific titles in Matt. 23. 8–11). Likewise, in John 21, an appendix to the gospel, the status given to Peter is an attempt to integrate Johannine tradition with that of the universal Church,[15] but without stipulation for a structural change in the Johannine communities. If the Lord should want John to continue till he comes, that is to be no concern of Peter (John 21. 22).

Clearly, the movement into the post-apostolic period involved the development of "offices" in the Church. These offices were structures which tended of their own nature to express authority. As stable components of the social fabric, they possessed an existence of their own which could give rise to a succession of persons exercising them. The office-holder in the Church, even beyond the respect and obedience his personal qualifications might command, could appeal to the authority of his office itself. As a paradigm, we may cite the development in the churches under Paul's influence. He appeals to the Corinthians to obey Stephanas and such others as work with him and manifest his dedication (1 Cor. 16. 15–16). The obvious signs of God's grace in their ministry should command obedience. When Paul addresses the bishops and deacons at Philippi, it is not clear that there has been any significant structural development beyond that noted at Corinth. These titles probably represent "functions" in the Church, that is, ministries exercised more in virtue of the personal qualities of the ministers than because of their occupying a socially acknowledged position bearing authority of itself. However, by the time these titles recur in the Pastorals, they represent stable offices in the Church. They are positions to which one can aspire (1 Tim. 3. 1) and for which one must give evidence of suitable preparation (1 Tim. 3. 6, 10).

[13] This scribe is acknowledged as a leader in the local community by R. Dillon, "Ministry as Stewardship of the Tradition in the New Testament", *Catholic Theological Society of America Proceedings* 24 (Yonkers, 1969), p. 43.

[14] R. Pesch, "The Position and Significance of Peter in the Church of the New Testament", *Concilium*, April 1971 (American Edn., Vol. 64).

[15] W. Trilling, *op. cit.*, 132.

However, "function" and "office" are not a simple dichotomy expressing a contrast between a genuine Spirit-filled authority and a human presumption to structure and channel the divine. In 1 Tim. 1. 18, the words of prophecy spoken with respect to Timothy's ordination, however they functioned in the actual situation, are a clear sign that the movements of the Spirit were still being discerned with regard to the exercise of authority. Surely the very demand that prospective officers give evidence of sustained fidelity to obligations was itself an attempt to establish the workings of God's grace in the candidate. To regard, however, such a structural development as narrowing down the charismatic fullness of the earlier Pauline church[16] is a one-sided view which, in the first place, does not take seriously enough the new situation of the Church, which sought to secure stability in the fact of waning eschatological expectation and of emerging theologies seen as dangerous to the tradition. Secondly and more basically, such a view seems to arise out of a perspective sceptical of human co-operation in God's salvific work. To imply that authority in the Church is to be legitimated by nothing more than the effects it produces (the sign of its charismatic power)[17] is in effect to deny to the Church the authority to structure itself anew in human fashion to meet new human situations. Catholic tradition of the union of human and divine in the Incarnation would favour understanding the bestowal of charismatic gift and the development of office as a fruitful interaction (note in Eph. 4. 11–12 the charismatic character of church development and the approximation towards the situation of the Pastorals).

Nothing in the New Testament directly opposes such an understanding and the development within the New Testament itself supports it. If Paul ascribes all ministries in the Church to the activity of the Spirit,[18] it is difficult to imagine that he could have characterized the development of "office" in the Church as anything other than a gift of this same Spirit. Thirdly,

[16] Cf. H. von Campenhausen, *op. cit.*, 74–5; E. Käsemann, "Ministry and Community in the New Testament", *Essays on New Testament Themes* (Studies in Biblical Theology 41) (Naperville, 1964), 89, 92 (*Exegetische Versuche und Besinnungen*,² Göttingen, 1960).

[17] E. Käsemann, *ibid.*, 70.

[18] *Ibid.*, 69–70, 72.

such a theology sceptical of human structures of authority is in part a reaction against abuses in the Catholic Church evidenced specially before the Reformation, and as such it is a caution that church office can never have a power exercised without an intrinsic and essential relationship to the gospel, the saving mission of Christ. This lack of autonomy in all church authority is at the heart of its distinction from any purely secular form (Luke 22. 25–26).

III. New Testament Church Order not a Fully-Developed System

Our preceding examination should not overlook those areas of the New Testament where (1) the conscious attitudes are not clear to us or (2) they are non-existent. Even such negative aspects of the New Testament picture can enrich our perspective as we ponder possible changes in church order. With regard to (1), the preceding investigation reveals numerous gaps in our information. We are usually not aware, of how church officers received their authority, to what extent ordination, even prior to the Pastorals, may have been involved. Even in the Pastorals, it is not clear how presbyter-bishops were chosen, if one grants that appointment by Timothy or Titus is a literary rather than an historical construction. The structure of the Matthaean church is unknown to us. Whether there were presbyters in the seven churches of the Apocalypse remains a question. The ascribing of royal power to the faithful in general (Apoc. 1. 6; 3. 21) no more excludes the presence of such officers than it did in 1 Peter (cf. 1 Pet. 2. 9; 5. 1).

Besides such examples, we can wonder about the role of the "leaders" in the Epistle to the Hebrews, how they relate to the earlier "leaders" who founded the church (Heb. 13. 7; compare verses 17, 24), and why in a conclusion so reminiscent of Paul such a title is used, even though it never appears in any of Paul's authentic letters. In short, the awareness of how frequently church structure is merely mentioned in passing leaves us in the dark about actual forms, but directs us to the fruitful and positive insight that the precise form of church order is generally not a central concern in the New Testament. We are thus forewarned against exaggerating the importance any individual form may be allowed to claim.

As for (2) above, the combination of various ecclesial orders into the single canon of the New Testament shows that church order shares in the non-systematic nature of the canon itself. Just as the canon contains varying theologies that have not been fully harmonized with each other, but which rather point the way towards further systematization, so the varieties of New Testament ecclesial order, by the fact of their incorporation into a single literary context, show the direction towards uniformity which later writings like the Pastorals express, but also disclose the unfinished and imperfect nature of the Church itself. For the canon expresses the basic nature of the Church and directs us to consider seriously an imperfection in that nature: the Church as existing in time and striving towards the fullness of Christ's promise. Thus, in the fact of the canon, we find a theological datum that probably goes beyond the intentions of those who gave the canon its final form: the Church's unfinished existence in history is intrinsic to its nature and expresses itself in the variability and imperfection of its structures. The canon has within itself the fluidity of the foundational period to which it witnesses; it invites us to ponder seriously our own developing historical situation and to acknowledge its condition of imperfect unity.

IV. THE ESSENTIAL BASIS OF CHURCH ORDER

The foregoing considerations, concerning a striving for unity and uniformity which builds upon a consciously accepted variety and culminates in a unity of the canon which does not submerge the variety of its components, prompts us to seek further the underlying reality which such development expresses. We find the basis for an answer in 1 Cor. 12, Paul's discussion of the various gifts which God bestows on his Church. In vv. 4–7, he calls them gifts, ministries, and works in order to express their variety and fullness[19] but indicates that they are all ordered towards man's relationship to the divine Persons. The subsequent

[19] K. Maly, *Mundige Gemeinde* (Stuttgarter Biblische Monographien 2) (Stuttgart, 1967), 188.

passage on the Body of Christ (12. 12–26) develops this idea specifically in a Christological direction. All is given to promote unity in Christ (cf. Eph. 4. 11–13). This same idea is also expressed in the closer relationship between church order and Paul's preaching of the gospel, to the point that both can be called "service" (*diakonia*); compare, e.g., Rom. 11. 13 and 1 Cor. 16. 15. The model is the service offered by Christ himself (cf. Mark 10. 45; Luke 22. 27; Paul does not apply the word *diakonia* directly to the mission of Christ himself, but implies as much in 2 Cor. 5. 19–20; 8. 4, 9, and perhaps in 1 Cor. 12. 5). By further implication, church office includes "gospel" within its essential structure. The strength of church office is thus at the same time its limitation: the service of a community that belongs to Christ (cf. 1 Cor. 3. 21–23).

This mark of genuine service remains a constant in the New Testament; for example, the bishops and deacons at Philippi are addressed second to the community (Phil 1. 1); the presbyters in 1 Peter and the presbyter-bishops in the Pastorals are like shepherds whose care must be for the flock. Also, the repeated joining of the commission of Peter together with mention of his misunderstanding or failure (Matt. 16. 18, 23; Luke 22. 32; John 21. 17) indicates human inadequacy for the task given by Christ and implies the presence of his power for a work beyond human strength (cf. 2 Cor. 4. 7–8). It is perhaps this very need to bind Peter's authority to the saving mission of Christ which prompted Matthew alone to present Peter as a foundation stone which is also a stumbling-block (Matt. 16. 18, 23). Such a description appears elsewhere applied to Christ (Matt. 21. 42, 44; Luke 20. 17–18; 1 Pet. 2. 7–8);[20] its application to Peter paradoxically suggests the presence of Christ's power in the authority of the weak and sinful office-bearer (cf. Matt. 28. 17, 20). A similar grounding of office in the mission of Christ is operative in the sending of the seventy-two in Luke 10, a foreshadowing of the Gentile mission (where Jews would now be free to eat what was set before them, Luke 10. 8) and perhaps even of the presbyteral office itself (with allusion to the seventy "presbyters" in Numbers

[20] This unique application to Peter is briefly noted by E. Schweizer, "Observance of the Law and Charismatic Activity in Matthew", *New Test. Stud.* 16 (1970), 222, but without any theological conclusions.

11). Also the multiplication of the loaves in Mark 6. 34–44 has several expressions strikingly reminiscent of church order concerns (shepherd motif, v. 34; emphasis on the participation of the disciples; allusion to the Christian eucharistic assembly, v. 41; groupings of hundreds and fifties, v. 40, recalling the commissioning of authorities in Exodus 18. 21); here too the role of church authorities is totally directed to the service Jesus wished to offer men.

V. Application to the Modern Situation

Having come thus far, we should find it relatively easy, at least from the viewpoint of New Testament considerations, to assess the legitimacy both of our present situation and of general prospects for the future. In fact, the responses become easier as one appreciates how limited an answer the New Testament can give to questions about present and future church order. We can best begin by stating the meaning of the scriptural canon for our problem.

The canon presents us with church order as determined largely by varying local situations, a fact which instructs us to regard the historical setting of the Church in the past, present and future as determinative of what church order should be. If so, we cannot expect to find clear answers to questions about possible new church orders from the New Testament alone. This is true not simply because we lack sufficient information about the original situation of the Church, but also because the need to take seriously the whole history of the Church demands that our relationship to the New Testament in this matter be one of dialogue, whereby we accept that the original period cannot be the same as any other and that therefore any attempt to be faithful both to it and to the modern age will permit that the New Testament give us only a partial answer.

The New Testament assigns to the Church the essential tasks of preaching the gospel and living in union with Christ through the sacraments. It also demands that church order be a service to both of these mandates in such a manner as to build up the unity of the Church. However, of itself, the New Testament makes no further absolute demands about particulars of struc-

ture, not even about such a matter as the reservation of sacramental functions to particular church officers. Such a conclusion
allows us to affirm calmly the legitimacy of the papal office even
though it does not appear as such in the New Testament. Similarly, if the "monarchical" episcopate is not present there (it
may be in the Pastorals, some argue,[21] and certainly the position
of James in Jerusalem appears close to such an office), it is likewise a development consonant with the New Testament striving
for stability in a still imperfect situation. Both these offices should
certainly not be called into question in the Roman Catholic
Church, for the general New Testament imperative to weigh
the historical situation does not allow us to jettison centuries of
experience with these orders that have so profoundly shaped the
Catholic tradition.

On the strength of the New Testament alone, other possibilities for church order besides the present-day papal and episcopal offices could have developed, but it seems naïve to establish them any more concretely than our study thus far has expressed them, precisely because their possibility is shaped by
the whole of church history, with special reference to the needs
of the present day. It is more fruitful to allow the New Testament
to engender in us an awareness of how little it imposes in matters
of church order. The potential universality of the gospel message requires that church order serve that universality and permit whatever variety of structures best fosters it. Moreover, we
can even consciously choose a variety of forms, even while striving to work out the gospel mandate for unity among the followers of Christ.

Not all forms need be part of a unified system nor even subject
to control of central authority; at least the New Testament shows
this is not absolutely necessary. For the sake of the gospel, the
experimental and non-systematic can be encouraged, within the
limitations imposed by the need to preserve and promote unity.
Church authorities, it seems, could best strengthen reverence for
their own position by promoting such freedom. Such a recommendation may bear its greatest fruit in the field of ecumenism,

---

[21] E.g., J. Gnilka, *op. cit.*, 100; A. Satake, *op. cit.*, 12. Contrary, N. Brox,
op. cit., 89.

where church order is being regarded as a potential aid rather than an obstacle to unity. The New Testament as a whole is supportive of the view that various Christian communions, even those without the episcopal order, can be reunited even while retaining their own structures, provided they reach agreement in basic truths of the faith and acknowledge the legitimacy of each other's ecclesial orders.[22] Such a reunion, without a subjection of all partners to the authority of the Pope, would indeed be imperfect, but it would follow the New Testament example of building church order upon the present situation and placing it at the service of the more basic reality which gives church order its meaning: Christ present in the preaching of the gospel, in the sacraments, in the life of the Church.

[22] The recommendation is that of R. Brown, *Priest and Bishop: Biblical Reflections* (New York, 1970), pp. 82-6.

Jean Colson

Ecclesial Ministries and the Sacral

FIRST of all, what is the "sacral"? We know, of course, that it is the opposite of the profane. But what precisely does this mean?

(1) According to religious thinking, there is a sacral space, perhaps a temple, which really exists only at the centre of profane space, the shapeless, chaotic expanse which surrounds the privileged space and which terrifies man as an image of nothingness.

Within this sacral space, it is possible for man to communicate with the transcendent, divine world. Here it is thought possible for man to make the ontological transition from one mode of being to another. Man thirsts for real existence and shows this thirst particularly in his desire to be at the centre of Being, in a place where he can communicate with the divine, draw near to it, and so exist as he was at the beginning when he left the hands of the creator.

(2) In addition to, and connected with this sacral space, we find in religions, in contrast to profane time which belongs to everyday experience and continues inexorably, the idea of sacral time, time in a stronger sense, pure time, primordial mystical time which does not move and which is made present by the regular celebration of feasts. This celebration is no more than an attempt to rediscover, by reviving it in the "historic" present through a repetition of the cosmogony, the sacral time in which the Deity, "in the beginning", before fleeting time, established the world and which in a way blends with the eternal.

This again is a wish on man's part to give the world the stability he dreams about but feels incapable of giving himself.

"Festivals" are like a "succession of eternities" in fleeting time, recovered by means of the reactualization of the primordial myth within the movement of the closed circle of a calendar and especially at the beginning of each new annual cycle. The sacral, then, is of cosmic significance.

(3) Just as there are sacral spaces and times there is also a sacral staff to preside over the rites. These men or women are set apart from the run of profane humanity and as a result "sacralized", placed in a unique relation with the divine world. Without them it is impossible to establish that communication with the divine world of which man dreams and where he hopes to set his being in a real, stable existence.[1]

When we come to Christianity the difference is obvious.

(1) In the first place, there is no "sacral" space, no privileged place within which, and only within which God can be met.

The Jews, of course, had a Temple in Jerusalem which they thought of as the "centre of the world". However, if we are to believe Stephen's preaching, building a house for God was King Solomon's mistake:[2] "The Most High does not dwell in houses made with hands; as the prophet says, 'Heaven is my throne, and earth my footstool. What house will you build for me, says the Lord, or what is the place of my rest? Did not my hand make all these things?' You stiff-necked people, uncircumcised in heart and ears, you always resist the Holy Spirit" (Acts 7. 47–51).

God had already opposed David's wish to build him a Temple: "Would you build me a house to dwell in? I have not dwelt in a house since I brought up the people of Israel from Egypt to this day . . ." (2 Sam. 7. 2 ff.). The prophets' view was that the Temple and its rites had never been wanted, but were merely tolerated by God as a result of "the basic lack of understanding of a people whose soul was idolatrous".[3]

---

[1] Cf. Mircea Eliade, *Traité d'Histoire des Religions* (Paris, 1968); "Das Heilige und das Profane", *Rowohlts Deutsche Enzyklopädie* (Hamburg, 1957—French translation, *Le sacré et le profane*, Paris, 1965).

[2] See also Josephus, *Antiquities* VIII, iii: "My friends", said Jeroboam, "I am sure that you realize that God is everywhere, and that there is no place in which he cannot hear the prayers and grant the requests of those who call on him."

[3] Cf. P. Prigent, *L'Epître de Barnabé I–XVI, et ses sources* (Paris, 1961).

And to the Samaritan woman puzzled about the authentic place where one could be sure of meeting God—"Our fathers worshipped on this mountain; and you (Jews) say that Jerusalem is the place where men ought to worship"—Jesus declared, "Woman, believe me, the hour is coming when neither on this mountain nor in Jerusalem will you worship the Father. . . . The hour is coming, and now is, when true worshippers will worship the Father in spirit and truth, for such the Father seeks to worship him. God is spirit, and those who worship him must worship in spirit and truth" (John 4. 20–24).

"Where two or three are gathered in my name, there am I in the midst of them", was Jesus' promise to his disciples (Matt. 18. 20). Christians are "living stones" to be "built into a spiritual house, to be a holy priesthood, to offer spiritual sacrifices acceptable to God through Jesus Christ", the corner-stone of believers (1 Pet. 2. 4 ff.). The Apostle Paul asked: "What agreement has the temple of God with idols? For we are the temple of the living God; as God has said, "I will live in them and move among them ' " (2 Cor. 7. 16). In the fourth gospel, the glory of God is revealed in Jesus Christ, the eternal Word of God made flesh (John 1. 14). For those who believe in him he is the "place" of meeting between men and God (John 2. 18–22).

Christians therefore do not build "temples" or sacral places for "the divine Power" to dwell in, but "churches", meeting-places where those who believe in Jesus Christ come together. Jesus Christ is the foundation stone of the spiritual temple which the believers together make up and in which the Spirit of God reveals himself.

(2) In the second place, as Mircea Eliade has observed, "Christianity has revived the experience and the concept of liturgical time by affirming the historicity of the person of Christ. For the believer the liturgy unfolds in *historical time sanctified by the incarnation of the Son of God*. The sacred time periodically made present again by the pre-Christian religions is a *mythical time* and primordial and cannot be identified with the historical past. It is an *original time* in the sense that it sprang up 'all at once' and was not preceded by any other time because no time could exist *before the appearance of the reality described by the myth*" (*Le sacré et le profane*, p. 53).

Later in the same work (pp. 96–7), he says: "In comparison with archaic and palaeo-oriental religions, and with the mythico-philosophical conceptions of the Eternal Return as they were developed in India and Greece, Judaism presents an innovation of major importance. *For Judaism time had a beginning and will have an end.* The idea of cyclical time is left behind. Yahweh will no longer reveal himself in *cosmic time* (like the gods of other religions), but in irreversible historical time. . . .

"Christianity goes even further in giving value to *historical time.* Because God has become *incarnate*, has taken on a *historically conditioned existence*, history becomes capable of being sanctified. The *illud tempus* mentioned by the gospels is a clearly defined time in history, the time when Pontius Pilate was governor of Judea, *sanctified by the presence of Christ.* The modern Christian who becomes part of liturgical time re-enters the *illud tempus* in which Jesus lived, suffered and rose, but this is no longer seen as a mythical time, but as the time when Pontius Pilate was governor of Judea. For the Christian also the sacred calendar takes up indefinitely the same events of the existence of Christ, but these events took place in history. They are no longer events which took place at *the origin of time*, but 'in the beginning' (with the nuance that, for the Christian, time begins again with the birth of Christ, because the incarnation establishes a new situation for man in the cosmos). In short, history reveals itself as a new dimension of the presence of God in the world. . . . It is to a theology, and not a philosophy, of history that Christianity gives rise. The reason is that the interventions of God in history, and above all the incarnation in the historical person of Jesus Christ, have a trans-historical object, the *salvation* of man."

(3) It follows from this that the relation between the ministerial leaders and the Christian "sacral" is no longer of the same type as that between "priests" (*hiereis-sacerdotes*) and the pagan "sacral". First of all, it is the whole fellowship of believers, based by faith on the corner-stone, Christ, and forming a spiritual temple, a priesthood, who "declare the wonderful deeds of him who called you out of darkness into his marvellous light" (1 Pet. 2. 9).

What are these wonderful deeds? They are the life and teaching and the death and resurrection of Jesus Christ. "For there is no other name under heaven given among men by which we must be saved" (Acts 4. 12). This is the definition of the relationship of the ministerial leaders to the Christian "sacral" given by the Apostle Paul in his Epistle to the Romans, where the proclamation of the Good News is described as "spiritual worship" rendered by the apostle to God (Rom. 1. 9). In the same epistle, Paul also speaks of "the grace given me by God to be a minister (literally, "liturgist") of Christ Jesus to the Gentiles in the *sacral function* (*hierourgounta*) of the gospel of God, so that the *offering* of the Gentiles may be *acceptable, sanctified* by the Holy Spirit" (Rom. 15. 16, RSV adapted).

The title *hiereus* is carefully avoided, to prevent any confusion with the Jewish, and still more with the pagan, *hiereis*. The terms used, however, clearly deliberately, show that the apostolic ministry of proclaiming the Good News is envisaged as having "sacral" status, from the fact that its object is to form a people saved in Jesus Christ and capable as a result of revealing that salvation to the world in its life.

Thus the ministerial leaders are also seen, again by the Apostle Paul, as the architects of the spiritual temple: "According to the commission of God given to me, like a skilled master builder I laid a foundation, and another man is building upon it. Let each man take care how he builds upon it. For no other foundation can anyone lay than that which is laid, which is Jesus Christ. . . . Do you not know that you are God's temple and that God's Spirit dwells in you? . . . God's temple is holy, and that temple you are" (1 Cor. 3. 10–11, 16–17).

The "priests" belonging to the religions were in a sense "at God's side", or in other words "sacral" beings, as a result of having been dedicated, consecrated to a "sacral" place, where the divine was revealed or a "hierophany" took place. They were magi, with the task of re-creating mythical time within profane time and so establishing communication between men and the divine. They thus appear as intermediaries between the deity and men.

Something of this remained in the Jewish priesthood, but nothing is left in the Christian ministerial leaders: "for there is one God, and there is one mediator between God and men, the man Christ Jesus, who gave himself up as a ransom for all" (1 Tim. 2. 5–6). And the ministerial leader is simply "appointed a preacher and apostle, . . . a teacher of the Gentiles" in respect of the "testimony which was borne at the proper time" (1 Tim. 2. 7, 6). The ministers are the "stewards of the mysteries of God" (1 Cor. 4. 1), those through whom God "spreads the fragrance of the knowledge of him everywhere" (2 Cor. 2. 14). They are "the aroma of Christ to God" (2 Cor. 2. 15–16). In other words, in place of the "fragrant" sacrifices once offered by the *hiereis*, the ministers of the New Covenant, through the preaching which arouses faith in Christ, send up from this world the fragrance of a spiritual offering from the believing people.

It is this which allows us to make a connection between the ministers of the New Testament and the priests of the Old. According to Deuteronomy, the latter had the task of sending "incense rising to the nostrils" of God, of "keeping the word" of God and of "holding firmly to his covenant" (Deut. 33. 10, 9, JB). It was for failing in this that they were criticized by the prophets, for not teaching the law in a way which would have reminded the holy people of their priestly character, thus causing them to give glory to God in the whole of their lives by behaving like "priests" (Hos. 4. 4 ff.; Jer. 2. 8; Mal. 2. 5–8). On the other hand, the Pauline definition makes any connection between the Christian minister and the pagan priests, whose only task was to watch over a "sacral" place and carry out "sacred" rites in it, out of the question. What is more, the title *hiereus*, applied to the minister in the Jewish and pagan priesthoods, is never used in the New Testament—or in the primitive sub-apostolic tradition—for a Christian minister.

The arguments of the Epistle to the Hebrews about Christ the priest—or high priest—are dominated by the idea that even the levitical priesthood has lost its status and that the only genuine mediation which exists between God and mankind in the messianic order is in the person of Jesus Christ, who was raised to the position of mediator in stages, first through his incarnation, then through his suffering and death on the cross and finally through his glorification, which is described as a fulfilment (Heb. 1. 3; 7. 23–25; 7. 13–14, etc.). This redemptive action as a whole is regarded as the sacrifice of the high priest of the New Covenant.

It is nevertheless clear from a reading of the relevant passages in Hebrews that traditional ideas of priesthood and sacrifice are transcended: "Every high priest chosen from among men is appointed to act on behalf of men in relation to God, to offer gifts and sacrifices for sins"; "He can deal gently with the ignorant and wayward, since he himself is beset with weakness"; "No one takes the honour upon himself, but he is called by God, just as Aaron was"; "So also Christ did not exalt himself to be made a high priest (*archiereus*), but was appointed by him who said to him, 'Thou art my Son, today I have begotten thee. . . . Thou art a priest (*hiereus*) for ever, after the order of Melchizedek.' . . . Although he was a Son, he learned obedience through what he suffered; and being made perfect he became the source of eternal salvation to all who obey him, being designated by God a high priest (*archiereus*)" (Heb. 5. 1–2, 4–5, 6, 8–10).

Their only function now is that of images, symbols, of a "grammar", as they have been called, to express the admission of man, in Jesus Christ, into the realm of the divine and eternal which he felt his way towards for so long in vain through the institutions of sacrifice and priesthood. Man has now entered at last and only because the Son of Glory (Heb. 1. 3–13) assumed, in his incarnation, leadership of humanity so that, glorified himself beyond death, he might admit man in his turn to that glory. Through him and with him and in him, at his resurrection, when he "rent the veil" between the divine world and the profane world, God has made all men pass through into the eternal sanctuary as in a forerunner (Heb. 6. 19–20).

The result of this is that Christ's "priesthood" tends ultimately towards the abolition of the difference between profane and sacral. Since in Jesus Christ God has pitched his tent—his temple —among us, in the midst of us, as the fourth gospel says, and we have seen in him the glory of God (John 1. 14), communion with the divine is no longer limited to one place or time or to a privileged few, but is in the process of being extended to the whole of the new priestly human race. "Go", said the risen Christ to his apostles, "and make disciples of all nations. . . . I am with you always, to the close of the age" (Matt. 28. 19–20). It is for this reason that the title *hiereis* was never given to Christian ministers, and it would also be wrong to attribute to them what is said of Christ the *hiereus*. This title is, however, given to all the believers baptized in Jesus Christ (Rev. 6. 9–11; cf. 1. 13), and more particularly to those who have borne witness to their faith by death (Rev. 20. 4–6). And the believers, the baptized, as a whole, form in Jesus Christ a *hierateuma*, a priestly people (1 Pet. 2. 5–9).

This abolition of the distinction between the "sacral" and its taboos on the one hand and the profane on the other is clearly stated by the Apostle Paul. What does it matter whether or not the meat one buys in the market has been offered to idols! "Eat whatever is sold in the meat market without raising any question on the ground of conscience. For 'the earth is the Lord's, and everything in it.' . . . If I partake with thankfulness, why am I denounced because of that for which I give thanks? So, whether you eat or drink, or whatever you do, do all to the glory of God." But if all things are lawful, "not all things are helpful. 'All things are lawful', but not all things build up." Thus it may be necessary "for conscience' sake" to refrain from eating meat which is offered to you by someone who tells you, "This has been offered in sacrifice": "I mean his conscience not yours", explains the apostle (1 Cor. 10. 23–31) "As for the man who is weak in faith, welcome him, but not for disputes over opinions. One man believes he may eat anything, while the weak man eats only vegetables. Let not him who eats despise him who abstains, and let not him who abstains pass judgment on him who eats; for God has welcomed him. . . . One man esteems one day as better than another, while another man esteems all days alike. Let every one be fully convinced in his own mind. He who observes the day, observes it in honour of the Lord. . . . I know and am persuaded in the Lord Jesus that nothing is unclean in itself —this is the idea of clean and unclean which is intimately connected with the idea of the sacral—but it is unclean for anyone who thinks it unclean. If your brother is being injured by what you eat, you are no longer walking in love" (Rom. 14. 1–15).

It is in this sense—"I speak", says Paul, "as to sensible men" (1 Cor. 10. 14)—that "you cannot drink the cup of the Lord and the cup of demons. You cannot partake of the table of the Lord and the table of demons" (1 Cor. 10. 21).

Finally, the New Testament idea of holiness, of the "sacral", is summed up in a fundamental passage in 1 Peter:

"As he who called you is holy, *be holy yourselves in all your conduct*; since it is written, 'You shall be holy, for I am holy'. ... So *put away all malice and all guile and insincerity and envy and all slander.* ... You are a chosen race, a royal *priesthood*, a *holy* nation, ... that you may declare the wonderful deeds of him who called you out of darkness into his marvellous light" (1 Pet. 1. 15–16; 2. 1; 2. 9).

In short, the sacralization of man has its origin in the sanctification by the Spirit (1 Pet. 1. 2), the new birth "of imperishable seed, through the living and abiding *word* of God" (1 Pet. 1. 23). Its crown is obedience to the truth, to the word which is the Good News which was preached to us and which was summed up in the "law of holiness" of Leviticus: "Love one another" (1 Pet. 1. 25; 1. 23; 1. 22; cf. Lev. 19. 18). This is the law of the "sacral" in the lives of Christians.

It is the task of Christians to grow towards salvation, not in isolation but in community, as a people ordained, "sacralized", by faith in the word of God. That is the reason for the rite of the breaking of bread—"The bread which we break, is it not a participation in the body of Christ? Because there is one bread, we who are many are one body, for we all partake in the one bread"—and also the reason why breaking bread in division, in a state of sin against fraternal charity, means that a man "eats and drinks judgment upon himself" because "he eats and drinks without discerning the body" (1 Cor. 10. 16–17; 11. 17–22; cf. 10. 14–31). This rite is therefore not "sacral" in the same way that the religions understood the term, but a statement, a proclamation of the death of the Lord who, by dying, has sanctified mankind and made them "a royal priesthood, a holy nation, a people for his possession", so that by its actions they may bear witness to the marvellous deeds—the death and glorification of the Saviour—performed by God for their sake (1 Cor. 11. 26; 1 Pet. 2. 9).

This is the "spiritual worship" required of Christians, "to present your bodies as a living sacrifice, holy and acceptable to

God. Do not be conformed to this world but be transformed by the renewal of your mind, that you may prove what is the will of God, what is good and acceptable and perfect" (Rom. 12. 1–2). But what is it then that gives the ministry a "sacral" status, in the sense which the word can be given in New Testament thought, and not, of course, in the "religious" sense? What gives it that status is the primordial function of the Christian ministry, to gather men together in faith by the proclamation of the Good News of Christ dead and risen and make mankind as a whole "sacramental", a witness in its life to the holiness of God who made it holy in Jesus Christ.

But in that case what difference is there between the proclamation of the gospel by an authorized minister and that made by any believer? The difference is that the first is a proclamation by an "official" representative of Christ, in the name of Christ himself, to call together and establish the *holy* people. And the *order* which confers this ministry is a sacrament because it establishes the ministers as *signs*—effective signs—that the word of God by which men are called together to form the Church, the company of the saints, is an initiative of God's, a gift of God, a grace, and that men of themselves cannot hear the word which brings them together. As Paul says, "How are they to believe in him of whom they have never heard? And how are they to hear without a preacher? And how can men preach unless they are sent?" (Rom. 10. 14–15).

This announcement in God's name of his wonderful deeds in Jesus Christ for the sake of men is made not only by preaching but also ritually, at the Lord's Supper, by which the participants "proclaim the death of the Lord until he comes" (1 Cor. 11. 26). If it is the function of the appointed minister to preside at this "supper", this is not in virtue of any "sacral" character of the same type as in the religions, in which priesthood appears as separated from the profane and dedicated, in a sacral place and a sacral time, to sacral rites in the way which has been described, but because it is fitting for the one who summons, establishes and completes the people of the saints by the preaching of the wonderful deeds of God should also complete the people by presiding at the meal which ritually announces those deeds.

Here again, the minister is a sign that it is not the people which has been summoned which can put into action, in the eucharistic meal, its own redemption and give itself the grace of taking part in it. This Christological element in the ministry, in the ministry of word and sacrament, is fundamentally a sign of the need for the mediation of Christ, the one mediator.

Clearly, this view of the ministry is quite different from the sort of "sacralization"—in the sense of the old religions—of church functions which results in their clericalization, that is, in their being regarded as forming a sort of "sacral" caste within the Christian people, more or less separate from it and dedicated to "sacral" acts in a "sacral" place and "sacral" time.

Some "declericalization" of the Christian ministries can therefore only be a purification. The temple of God is wherever two or three are gathered in the name of Christ, who is then in the midst of them. But the group must meet or be summoned in the name of Christ, and it is from this that the ministry which summons, assembles and completes the believers in the name of Christ—in persona Christi—receives its meaning as a sign. The minister is a sign that the gathering is not a merely human gathering, but a summons by God's grace to believe in his love, the love of which he gave a pledge in the wonderful deeds he performed in Jesus Christ and of which the ministers are no more than official heralds by preaching and ritual.

Translated by Francis McDonagh

Alexandre Ganoczy

"Splendours and Miseries" of the Tridentine Doctrine of Ministries

THE Council of Trent set out to remedy a crisis which it considered a disorder. It was seeking to ensure that the "hirelings" within and the "wolves" without could no longer threaten the Church.[1] To this end, the Council had recourse to as clear and traditionally based a theology as possible, and to disciplinary measures. Within the perspective of restoration and defence it seemed indispensable for the ministries of the Church once again to form a true *acies ordinata*.[2] Thus, if the play on words may be excused, Trent rethought the sacrament of order to restore order in the Church.

History has recognized that this immense enterprise, which some call the Catholic "restoration" and others the Catholic "reformation", was a more or less valid and effective reply to Lutheran and Calvinist questions and challenges. But it has also recognized that in the course of the following four centuries a too rigid desire to stick to the letter of the Council has sometimes blocked the progress which ought to have taken place within the structures of the Church, in response to new challenges and questions. Today, following the reforming experience of Vatican II, we are in a position to ask what was the profound cause underlying this state of affairs, why Trent was

[1] Cf. A. Duval, "L'ordre au Concile de Trente", *Etudes sur le sacrement de l'ordre* (Lex Orandi 22, Paris, 1957; quoted henceforth as "Duval"), pp. 279 and 286.
[2] Denzinger–Schönmetzer, *Enchiridion Symbolorum et Definitionum* ("DS"), 1767.

able to give only a partial response to the questions raised by
Protestantism concerning the Church's ministries, and why its
decrees were incapable of inspiring a continual doctrinal and
disciplinary evolution in this field. The question as we have
posed it may seem too negative and critical. This would be the
case if it were not asked with the firm purpose of achieving
objectivity, that is, in a *total* picture of both the positive and
negative aspects of the Tridentine tradition, whether of reformation, non-reformation or counter-reformation. We shall in
fact attempt to draw up such an objective balance-sheet within
the limits of a schematic presentation.

But since we are attempting a schematic presentation of complex facts and ideas, we shall begin by indicating our reply to
the question we have raised. It seems that all the inadequacies
of the Council and of the tradition which derived from it have
as their principal cause the absence of a true *theology of the
Word*, a theology which should have formed the hermeneutic
principle for its statements concerning the ministry, and to
have set in motion a continually reforming interpretation of
them. There is some confirmation of this hypothesis when one
considers that the power of the Protestant Reformation was
drawn largely from the principle *solum verbum*. This principle
dominated the Christological, soteriological and ecclesiological
doctrine of the Reformers, and also supplied a hermeneutic
principle for their doctrine of the sacraments and the ministry.
A more modern confirmation can be found in the fact that by
developing a particular theology of the Word, Vatican II succeeded in providing a basis for the priority which is accorded
to the ministry of preaching, teaching and witness in the context of an integral ecclesiology. Hence the conclusion which by
now has become evident: the true theological dialogue between
Luther and Rome did not take place until Vatican II.

Ought things to have been different? Indeed they ought. But
could they have been different? That is difficult to say. There
are in fact good grounds for thinking that the Lutheran theology of the Word, in the form that it took at that period, with
its polemic assertions, its one-sided emphases and its sometimes
anarchic practical results (e.g., the *Schwärmer*) could not have
been listened to by a Church which had taken as its funda-

mental aim the re-establishment of order in its ranks and continuity with its tradition. Hence the paradoxical but not absurd
concluson, that it was perhaps only by refusing to "swallow
whole" the Lutheran theology of the *Verbum* that Trent was
able to match up to its immediate task. Whether Catholic
theologians were right to maintain this refusal for four centuries is another question.

In the considerations which follow, we shall try to outline
some important aspects of the Tridentine doctrine of the ministry, and to identify some of the causes and some of the consequences of it.

1. *The Principle of Functionality.* The Reformers never
ceased to castigate the Roman practice of conferring an order
upon someone who was sure that he would never exercise it,
either because he was incapable of it, or because the order in
question no longer corresponded to a real function. The Reformers habitually illustrated this lack of seriousness by the
example of the minor orders, which in their eyes were empty
vestiges of a past era. Catholic theologians such as Peter de Soto
and John Gropper were not insensitive to this charge.[3] While
they were in favour of the maintenance of the minor orders,
they wished them to be no longer conferred to no purpose, but
to correspond to real, serious and useful functions. This wish is
expressed in the projected decree of the 7th July 1563, which
gave a long description of the indispensable tasks in the current pastoral situation: the visiting of the sick, catechizing,
charitable work and administration, tasks which could be
allotted for example to exorcists, readers subdeacons and
deacons.[4] In the same sense, and a year earlier, a commission
of five Italian bishops called for priests with no work to do to
be assigned to the exercise of the minor orders, restored to significance in this way.[5] One may regret that the final decree *De
reformatione* of the 15th July 1563 did not go as far as these
concrete propositions, limiting its directives to the field of worship,[6] and that the dogmatic decree of the same date presented
the existence of a number of orders as no more than an element

---

[3] Cf. Duval, pp. 308 f.   [4] *Concilium Tridentium* ("*CT*"), IX, 598–601.
[5] *CT* XIII, 608, 12 and 29.
[6] *Conciliorum Oecumenicorum Decreta* ("*COD*"), 726, 8–24.

of dignity and veneration in the practice of public worship, and minor orders as no more than stages in the ascent towards the priesthood.[7] If the Council had been inspired by an authentic theology of the Word, it would have achieved results here which would have been both more theological and more practical; a number of ministries as a consequence of the diverse incarnation of the gospel according to the real needs, actual functions and therefore usefulness required of each order in the service of the creative Word, and the element of proclamation and witness in even the most material form of service,[8] etc.

Another aspect of functionality was more fully expressed at the Council: the importance of the *intention* of the minister in the exercise of his mission. On this point Trent proclaims that the quality of the action of the Church is more important than the intellectual or moral quality of the agent.[9] Whether the priest has progressed far in sanctity or is in a state of sin, he always acts in the name of God and of the Church, as long as he takes seriously the purpose of his action. He is a steward. What he does is *alieni beneficii dispensatio*.[10] Even if he is in a state of mortal sin, his action, carried out as the action of the Church, is valid in the sight of God and the faithful.[11] In this case, to paraphrase Luther, he is *simul peccator et minister Dei*. No Donatist perfectionism! The sanctifying holiness of the Word is more important than the dignity of him who proclaims it. Ought one not to see in this an act of trusting faith in the God of the *justificatio impiorum*, as well as a condemnation of all individualism, destructive of community, on the part of a minister? And is there not a hint here of the profound reflection of Vatican II, that every action of the Church is a service?

2. *The sacramentality* of order, as it is defined by Trent, is set in a similar theocentric and ecclesiological context, although it is palpably different from the functional thought outlined above. The very insistence upon the fact that ordination and order constitute a sacrament *in fieri et in esse* is completely explained by the desire to make a clear affirmation of the *specific*

[7] DS 1765 and 1772.
[8] See the discussion by Calvin of the social diaconate, in A. Ganoczy, *Calvin, théologien de l'Eglise et du ministère* (Paris, 1964), pp. 381–6.
[9] DS 1611 f.   [10] DS 1685.   [11] DS 1710.

nature of the institutional ministry in relation to the services which all Christians can supply.[12] Here there is agreement with a concern of Calvin, who regarded it as an abuse to appeal, for example, to the royal priesthood as a reason for according to everyone without distinction the responsibility for the Word and the sacraments. For, he said, "there is an express command of Jesus Christ to ordain certain ministers specially for this purpose".[13] Elsewhere he says that "it is a perverse thing for a private person to undertake to administer baptism or the Lord's Supper".[14] Better still, the French Reformer goes as far as to contemplate recognizing ordination as a true sacrament, on condition that it is used to create ministers of the Word and not "sacrificers".[15] He will not hear of *sacerdotes*, nor of any *character indelibilis* imprinted upon their soul, for in his view the aim of ordination is not an ontological consecration to the priesthood, but only the functional service of the word of God in the form of preaching and sacrament.

The Council, on the other hand, defends just as energetically the specific nature of the institutional ministry as an *acies ordinata*,[16] and does so by returning to the scholastic theory of the indelible mark which makes it impossible for a Christian, once ordained, to become a layman again.[17] In view of the narrowness of this view, some critics of Tridentine doctrine consider themselves justified in saying that here a juridical provision is propped up by an ontological fiction, while in Calvin there is a coherent theology of the Word, which requires a specific functional distinction and, as a consequence, a juridical distinction. This criticism is no doubt somewhat over-simplified. Be that as it may, it continues to give Catholic apologetics a good deal to think about, particularly at a period when "reductions to the lay state" are multiplying to a considerable extent. Thus an effort is being made nowadays to interpret the doctrine of sacerdotal character more adequately.[18]

3. In spite of the reserves that seem appropriate on this last point, we must recall that Trent did not attempt to base the

---

[12] DS 1766 f.   [13] *Opera Calvini ("OC")*, 7, 496.
[14] *OC* 4, 929 = *Institutio* II.15.20.   [15] *OC* 4, 1118 f. = *Institutio* IV.19.31.
[16] DS 1610, 1684, 1697, 1719, 1767.   [17] DS 1767, 1774.
[18] E.g., W. Kasper, in *Concilium*, March 1969 (American Edn., Vol. 43), and E. Ruffini, *ibid.*, Jan. 1968 (American Edn., Vol. 31).

authority of institutional ministers upon the sacramental nature of order alone. It paid equal regard to the intellectual *competence* and spiritual quality which ministers ought to possess. Consequently there were numerous discussions on the training of the clergy. The background to these debates was the founding by Protestants of numerous theological colleges which succeeded very well in bridging the abyss between university teaching and preparation for the pastoral ministry,[19] the setting up of seminaries by Reginald Pole in England and the desire shown by numerous theologians (Gropper, de Soto) and bishops to be equal at last to the intellectual competition of the Protestants. Unfortunately, most of the Council fathers were unable to look beyond the level of financial and moralizing considerations, with the result that canons 13, 14 and 18 of the *Decreta super reformatione* (1563) do no more than demand a minimum of knowledge from ordinands and present nothing like such a coherent and demanding programme of study as, for example, that of Calvin's Academy founded in Geneva in 1559.[20] Of course Calvin, a humanist Reformer, started from a truly theological conception of the ministry of the Word, and was consequently able to determine the respective importance of exegetical studies, patristics, the study of languages, and of systematic and practical theology in the training of ministers. There was nothing similar at the Council, which was content to legislate without at the same time indicating the profound significance and the normative structures of what was decreed. This explains why the real renewal in the training of the Catholic clergy was ultimately the work of an active minority (especially the Jesuits) and not the detailed and laborious application of the Tridentine decree.

4. At this point it is logical to ask whether the Council tackled the ministry of the Word as such. In this respect, it is instructive to examine the *Decretum super lectione et praedicatione*, which was voted upon on the 17th June 1546. The underlying problem was the proper way of defining the connection between

---

[19] Cf. A. Laurent, "L'influence du protestantisme sur l'origine des séminaires", *La pensée catholique* (1950), pp. 26–41; Duval, pp. 318 f.

[20] See A. Ganoczy, *La Bibliothèque de l'Académie de Calvin* (Geneva, 1969), pp. 133–55.

preaching and sacrament. According to Thomist tradition, it is the sacrament of sacraments, the Eucharist, which forms the centre of priestly activity. According to Thomas preaching is only a "remote preparation for the reception of the sacrament".[21] Under the joint pressure of Christian humanism and the Reformation, the proclamation of the Word was tending to gain priority at the very heart of the sacramental celebration. The Council of Cologne, held in 1536, decreed that every administration of a sacrament should be *accompanied* by some kind of preaching, so that the *faith* of the faithful might be illuminated by a true *understanding* of the mysteries being carried out.[22] It should be noted that this requirement, which was applied by Matteo Giberti to his diocese of Verona in 1543, corresponds exactly to what was required by Calvin in 1541 in his *Ordonnances ecclési-astiques*.[23] The decree of Trent of the 11th November 1563 finally incorporated this requirement.[24]

Meanwhile, however, a considerable number of Council fathers brought forward all kinds of reserves about the priority of preaching. The origins of the decree *Super lectione* make this clear. The projected decree of the 13th April 1546 is still inspired by a spirit of prophecy. It poses in an almost dramatic tone the problem of schools, and of the bishops' duty to evangelize.[25] In order that *young people*, and in particular those who are destined for the priesthood, might be properly in-structed, the authors of the projected decree wished to have available a well-based method of introduction to the reading of the Bible. In this context they raise the question of the "theology canon" and the Catechism. Secondly, they recall that it is the *bishops* who are responsible in the first instance for the pro-clamation of the gospel, which is the "*principal* foundation of the Christian religion". The bishops must carry out this essen-tial ministry personally and in all simplicity, every time they have the opportunity. (A necessary provision in view of the anarchy of "wandering" preachers.) This projected decree was

[21] Cf. J. Giblet, "Les prêtres" in G. Baraúna and Y. Congar, *L'Eglise de Vatican II*, vol. III ("Baraúna"; Paris, 1966), pp. 924 f.
[22] *Canones Concilii provincialis Coloniensis*, Verona, 1543, fol. 29–30, quoted by Duval, pp. 285 f.
[23] *OC* 10, pp. 103 f.
[24] *COD* 740, 13–25; Duval, p. 291.   [25] *CT* V, 105–108.

revised several times, and, it must be admitted, made more and more juridical at the expense of the spirit of prophecy. In the final version, one is struck by the numerous penalties threatened for those who neglect the "treasury of the sacred books", and by the somewhat didactic understanding of evangelization. It is regarded as a matter of handing on everything that one has to *know* (*scire*) to be saved. Once again, a theological basis and the profound underlying meaning of the duties imposed are cruelly lacking, as is a balanced appreciation of the relationship between faith and knowledge. In spite of all this, one decisive result was achieved: the affirmation that the preaching of the gospel is the *praecipuum munus*, the *primary* function of bishops.

Unfortunately, the subsequent work of the Council was marked by a series of retreats on this point. As early as 1547, the majority thought it more important to condemn the Lutheran thesis that the ministry consists only of the power of preaching and not that of sacrificing than to recall the duty of bishops and priests to teach. On this point, the amendments of Lippomani and Catharin in 1547 were as firmly rejected as those of Gropper and Seripando in 1563.[26] For fear of appearing too "Protestant", the Council in the end refused to develop the dogmatic content of its disciplinary declaration concerning the *praecipuum munus*. Its dogmatic decree on the priesthood was virtually to ignore the priority of preaching. It no longer mentions it except in the form in which it is to be condemned, that of the *nudum ministerium praedicandi*.[27] Would the Council have done this if it had had available a solidly based theology of the Word?

Indirectly at least, these retreats had two logical consequences: a lack of clarity on the subject of the "triple ministry" of bishops, and an excessive sacerdotalization of the ministry of priests. The lack of balance between the powers of the bishop with regard to teaching, the sacraments and discipline continually created theoretical and practical confusions during the centuries that followed Trent. Generally speaking, the priest was to appear above all as the man of the Mass. As for the bishop, it was possible for theologians as distinguished as Scheeben to teach that his power of teaching the Christians in his own diocese derives from his power of jurisdiction in the broader sense of the word,

[26] Duval, pp. 300, 302.   [27] DS 1767 and 1771.

because it consists of a "power of *imposing faith*"![28] Finally, we may point out that Vatican II, in spite of its efforts to clarify the triple ministry of the bishop, proved unable to remove every ground for the criticism that *in practice* this amounts to a "triple fiction". For, as critics ask, which bishop still teaches nowadays on his own account without *following* his theologian, who, however, does not belong to the teaching Church? And which bishop still manages to administer the sacraments except by the agency of other persons? Here a theology of "plenitude" and "infallibility" seems to stumble against the typically modern conditions of the seeking out and transmission of the truth. The idea of "supreme responsibility" is no longer sufficient in itself to be intellectually satisfying. Hence the numerous misunderstandings concerning the effective mission of bishops and priests. All this brings us back to our initial question: if the Council of Trent had succeeded in centring the whole of its doctrine of the ministry on a dynamic theology of the *Verbum*, would not this theology have been capable today of integrating, for example, the typically modern category of *dialogue* in the theory of the mediatory function of the Church?

5. The other consequence of the hesitations of Trent is unquestionably an excessive *sacerdotalization* of the ministry. The linguistic and historical problem associated with the terms *hierus* and *hierateuma* do not seem even to have occurred to the Council fathers. Thus it is easy to understand that their programme did not include a clarification of the distinction between *sacerdotium* and *ministerium*, in spite of the questions posed by the Reformers. Nevertheless, such a clarification would have been a logical consequence of the doctrine *de Missae sacrificio* promulgated in 1562. There, the uniqueness of the priesthood of Christ was perfectly related to the ministerial and representative priestly function which is attributed to the apostles and their successors, bishops *and* (the context allows us to say) priests.[29] But once again the haste to condemn the error of the opposition overcame any constructive concern. The *Doctrina de sacramento ordinis* promulgated in 1563 no longer re-

[28] J. M. Scheeben, *Handbuch der katholischen Dogmatik* I (Freiburg, 1948), pp. 74 f.; cf. J. Lecuyer, "La triple charge de l'evêque", in Baraúna, p. 896.   [29] DS 1739–1741, 1752.

turns to the theme of the unique sacrifice of Christ. It makes a doubtful and accommodating exegesis of Heb. 7. 12 ff., and seems preoccupied solely with defending the hierarchical priesthood against the Protestant thesis of the universal priesthood. 1 Peter 2. 9 ff. is not even mentioned. And as there is no theology of the Word there to supply a hermeneutic unity amongst the different statements of the Council, priesthood is defined in a one-sided way in terms of its sacrificial and sacramental function, as a power of consecrating, offering and administering the Eucharist, and of absolving from sins. A general reference to the Bible has to suffice to justify this approach.[30] There is no positive mention of a preaching mission, previously stated to be primary.

This one-sided sacerdotalization and sacralization of the ministry persisted for four centuries without being challenged by Catholic theologians. We must concede, of course, that they made possible a striking renewal of eucharistic devotion and of the mystique of the priesthood. It was Vatican II, with its opening in an ecumenical direction, which first modified these perspectives, precisely to the degree to which it placed a new emphasis upon the royal priesthood of all believers and placed the ministerial priesthood "at the point of contact between the sacrifice of Christ and that of the faithful".[31] But the balance obtained in this way seems to have been lost sight of once again in the doctrinal summary drawn up for the *Synod* of bishops at Rome in 1971. A remarkable confusion can be observed in it between "ministerial priesthood" and "priestly ministry". This is serious, not only from the ecumenical point of view, but also with regard to the increasing secularization of the world which has to be evangelized. The question in fact arises whether the concept of priesthood is still the most appropriate for translating for the benefit of our contemporaries the reality of the Church's ministry, as it is revealed in the gospel message. Ought one not rather to look amongst concepts such as *diakonia*, mission or witness, in order to avoid our ministries being seen as purely cultic functions? The priority of the *missionary* aspect of the proclamation of the *Verbum* in word and in act seems to supply the most adequate critical factor here, since it is both

[30] DS 1764.   [31] Giblet, p. 931

clearly attested by the New Testament and intelligible to modern man.[32]

6. It would be an anachronism to expect the Council of Trent to have the same type of missionary outlook as has developed in those of our churches situated in a secularized and democratized environment. Thus it is understandable that Trent should not have called for a collegial and synodal co-ordination of the papal, episcopal, presbyteral and lay ministries such as is being worked out at the present day. The situation at that time undoubtedly required the reaffirmation of the hierarchy in the strict sense, with the relationships of subordination which this implies. It is within this perspective that Trent sought a middle way between, on the one hand, papalism and Gallicanism,[33] and between "presbyterian" and "episcopalian" tendencies on the other hand. "Is the episcopate of divine institution or not? Does the jurisdiction of bishops derive directly from Christ? What is the role of the Pope in its transmission? How is the superiority of the episcopate over the priesthood to be defined? Is the episcopate *verus et proprius ordo*, conferred by a *verum sacramentum*? Is the true concept of the *sacerdos* realized in the simple priest or in the bishop? ... All these questions were raised in the scholarly and passionate debates of October 1562 to July 1563."[34]

As we know, Trent did not make a final pronouncement on the specific sacramentality of the episcopate, as Vatican II was to do later. The latent "presbyterianism" of certain Thomist theologians seems to have been the reason for this. Had not Thomas taught that "the priesthood of *priests* represents ... the fullness of the sacrament of order" because of its principally eucharistic task, and did he not regard the episcopate, by contrast, above all "in the perspective of the *rule* of Christ over the Church"?[35] It is not for nothing that a bishop cried out in open session: *Taceant thomistae!*[36] ... In view of the explosive nature of the debates and the threatened breach between certain bishops and certain theologians, the assembly finally contented itself with specifying that the bishop belongs *praecipue* to the

---

[32] Cf. Giblet, pp. 919–32.   [33] Cf. Duval, pp. 304 f., 307 f.
[34] Duval, pp. 305 f.; cf. *CT* IX, 71.44 and 72.30.
[35] Giblet, pp. 924 f.   [36] *CT* IX, 84, 1–7, quoted by Duval, pp. 310 f.

hierarchical order and that he is superior to priests, being the only one to possess the power of ordaining and confirming.[37] As a result, the "burning question"[38] was resolved only provisionally. It has arisen once again at the present day, with even greater urgency. Vatican II itself, working out a doctrine of the episcopate and omitting to add to it an equivalent document of the presbyterate, did not succeed in establishing the necessary balance for the healthy functioning of the mission. Thus the "burning question" continues to burn.

But there is a point at which at the present day one feels perhaps even more strongly that the doctrine of the ministry of the Council of Trent is open to improvement. This point is that of the laity. Failing a theology of the Word which makes it possible to understand the Church in its totality as a people of God *gathered together and gathering in*, the layman appears in it as no more than a non-clergyman, or as the incarnation of "temporal" realities. The minister is not seen as arising from the midst of the people but rather as descending into it. Lay people are given no more than an extremely limited role in the choosing of a minister.[39] There is no mention of charismata. Above all, the "relationship to the worldliness" of society which is now regarded as a specific *mission* of the layman[40] occurs nowhere in the programme, whereas Luther and Calvin already made it an important element in their ethical teaching. But it was easy for them: they were able to make use of a solidly based hermeneutic principle which made it possible for them to conceive even of a *ministerium* of the laity. Here again the promise of the future came from forces outside the Council, such as the *Oratorio del divino amore* of Gaetano of Thiene, in which clergy and laity were to collaborate in order to carry out "the work of the Word by every means", the primary concern being for the poor.[41]

Translated by R. A. Wilson

---

[37] DS 1768, 1777.   [38] Duval, p. 308.
[39] Cf. DS 1769, 1777. The *electus ab omni populo* of Hippolytus seems to have been completely forgotten (*Traditio apostolica* 2, ed. Botte, Paris, 1946, pp. 26 f.).
[40] See e.g., E. Schillebeeckx in Baraúna 1013-1033.   [41] Duval, p. 283.

Stephen Neill

The Necessity of Episcopacy:
Anglican Questions and Answers

THE English Reformation, like most things English, is very difficult for those who are not themselves English to understand. It
fits into no pattern other than its own; and, though it was naturally influenced by all the complex currents of the time, in its
most important points it was determined by the character of its
two chief architects, King Henry VIII and Archbishop Thomas
Cranmer. Both these remarkable men, for different reasons,
adopted the principle *quieta non movere*, the King because to
the end of his life he believed in the possibility of Catholicism
without the Pope, the Archbishop because he was a typical Cambridge man, who preferred never to move unless he felt solid
ground beneath his feet and was ever cautious in introducing
change.

This being so, many things survived the upheaval of the Reformation just because it had never occurred to anyone to question them. There always had been bishops, and there seemed to
be no reason why bishops should not always be a part of the
establishment of the Church of England, now separated from
Rome. There was, however, a good deal of questioning as to the
nature and purpose of the episcopal office.

I. THE HENRICIAN QUESTIONINGS

As part of the preparations for the work which appeared in
1543 as *The Necessary Doctrine and Erudition of a Christian
Man*, a number of questions was issued to bishops and doctors

of the Church. Those relating to episcopacy are relevant to the subject of this article. For four hundred years the kings of England had managed to get in most cases the bishops that they wanted, though it was agreed that a bishop could not take office without the consent and approval of the Pope. Now, however, that the King had declared the Pope to be no more than a foreign bishop without jurisdiction in England, from whom did the bishop derive his authority? There could be but one answer— from the Supreme Head, who claimed to be the source of all law and authority in his kingdom, the new Justinian who would declare to his people what they were to believe, and would have *his* bishops to help him carry this heavy responsibility for the spiritual health of his subjects.

Some of the questions set at this time are curiously revealing. On what authority did the apostles appoint bishops? Was this only a temporary measure, because in those early days there were no Christian kings? Is consecration necessary for a bishop? Or does the authority given him by the King suffice? If all the bishops and priests of a region were to die, should the Christian King make others to supply their place? Is it in order for the Christian Prince to teach and preach God's Word and to make and constitute priests? Naturally many and varied answers were given to these questions; the interesting thing is that they could be set out by authority in this form.

What the questions reveal is that the pastoral aspect of the episcopal office had almost completely lapsed in the Middle Ages: "The English bishop was far from being a benign father in God, who knew all his clergy and went round preaching in their churches;...the relation was mainly a legal one, and on the visitation he resembled the judge of the *Dies Irae*; he came *cuncta stricte discussurus*."[1] Only in the nineteenth century did the English bishop begin to free himself from the weight of this medieval inheritance. One of the few bishops of the sixteenth century who tried to exercise a pastoral ministry was John Hooper of Gloucester, the martyr under Queen Mary—and he found the sphere of this pastoral ministry, surprisingly, in his diocesan court.

[1] E. Jacob, *The Fifteenth Century* (Oxford, 1961), p. 272.

Bishops, then, there would be; but it was only the Elizabethan divines who would seek to find justification for their existence in the earliest records of the Church, rather than in the needs of kings and queens, needing help in the management and direction of the Church.

II. SEVENTEENTH-CENTURY CONTROVERSIES

After the execution of Charles I in 1649 by his rebellious subjects, many Englishmen spent long years of exile in France, Holland and elsewhere. What was to be their attitude to the Churches, Roman, Gallican and Protestant, with which they found themselves in constant contact? Anglicans were divided. In the later years of Elizabeth, Calvinist influence in the Church of England had been strong; but the followers of such men as Lancelot Andrewes and William Laud attached a much greater value to tradition, and in some ways approximated to the Catholic view of the Church.

Most of the Laudians refused to receive Communion in the Protestant Churches. Others, however, took a more generous view; they drew a distinction between the continental Churches which had lost episcopacy through no fault of their own (though Anglicans were almost unanimous in wishing that these churches might recover that blessed gift which they had lost) and the English dissenters who had wantonly rejected the godly order of the national Church. Such Anglicans had little hesitation in communicating with these Protestant Churches with which they agreed on so many matters of doctrine and which had retained a carefully ordered ministry though not of the episcopal pattern. Their attitude was correctly summed up by Archbishop Bramhall of Armagh (1594–1663) when he wrote that he and those who agreed with him did not deny to these non-episcopal Churches the nature of Churches, but did deny that they had the perfection of Churches, which was not to be had without the divine gift of episcopacy.

III. INDIAN ADVENTURES

The extension of English interests beyond the continent of Europe landed the English Church in a number of unforeseen difficulties. From the time of Sir Thomas Roe, the first English ambassador to the court of the Great Mogul (1615), the East India Company had sent out chaplains to minister to its servants in India, but always in inadequate numbers. As English power grew and the number of British residents increased, the authorities in South India adopted what seemed to them a natural expedient, and asked the German and Danish missionaries who from 1706 onwards had been active in Madras and south of it, to serve as chaplains both to their troops and to their civil stations. Thus it came about that Lutherans who had never received Anglican or episcopal orders (though some had been ordained by the Lutheran bishop of Zealand in Denmark) entered the service of the British Company and received handsome salaries from it. The great Christian Friedrich Schwartz, who served in India without a break from 1750 to 1798, was in the service of the Company, without prejudice to his missionary activities, for more than thirty years and died a very rich man. These good pietists, living so far from the contentions of Europe, set little store by denominational differences; they were prepared to use the English Liturgy and even to translate it into Tamil. The facts were of course well known in England; but the High Church Society for Promoting Christian Knowledge, which from 1713 onwards supported the missionary work in India, dexterously succeeded in not making an issue of the employment of these faithful men who lacked episcopal ordination; they saw at that time no hope of Anglican bishops for India, and were glad to make the best of a practically satisfactory though ecclesiastically irregular situation.

When the Church Missionary Society entered the field, almost all its early missionaries were likewise German pietists who lacked episcopal ordination. When the first Anglican bishop T. F. Middleton did at last arrive in India in 1814, he was naturally much perplexed by the presence of these missionaries; his handling of the problem was curiously English and pragmatic; he did not feel able to license the missionaries in Bengal, who were roving evangelists without parochial status; but when he came to South India and found such Germans as the eminent Pohle in charge of regularly organized congregations of Indian Christians, he had no hesitation in according to them a good Anglican licence.

Middleton's successor, the greatly loved Reginald Heber, caused a good deal of criticism by conferring on the outstanding convert Abdul Masih Anglican orders, though he had already received Lutheran ordination; he also re-ordained a number of the Lutheran missionaries. He explained his policy in a carefully written letter addressed to the Rev. Deccar Schmidt. When on his travels in Germany, he wrote, he had not hesitated to receive the Holy Communion from the well-established Churches of that region; and, if he ever returned to Europe, would revert to his earlier practice. But the Church in India was legally a part of the Church of England; by admitting to Anglican orders some who already had Lutheran orders, he was not raising any fundamental principle of validity, but simply acting to make more widely acceptable the ministrations of these brethren, especially in the chaplaincy churches, in which it was very doubtful whether one who had not received Anglican ordination could legally minister.

Heber was probably as near as could be to that non-existent creature, the typical Anglican. If asked whether episcopacy is necessary to the existence of the Church, Heber and his like would probably have answered that episcopacy is necessary in the same way as arms and legs are necessary to the normal functioning of the human body, but not necessary in the same sense as the brain or the heart, without which human life cannot continue to exist at all. Such Anglicans had no doubt that episcopacy had come into existence as part of the will of the Lord for his Church; but they did not for that reason think it necessary to deny all recognition to non-episcopal bodies in which the gifts of the Spirit were manifest, a pure gospel was preached, the sacraments ministered, and a regular church order maintained.

IV. Apostolic Succession

Anglicans of all schools of thought have always agreed in attaching a high value to episcopacy. But it seems that the rigid view that episcopacy is so necessary to the life of the Church that any non-episcopal body cannot be regarded as having any of the reality of the Church at all did not enter the Church of England earlier than 1833, the year generally recognized as having seen the beginning of the Oxford or Anglo-Catholic movement. John Henry Newman (1801–1890) still remains a somewhat enigmatic figure. His conversion had brought him into touch with Evangelicals, since these were the only earnest Christians of Anglican allegiance of whom he had any knowledge; but, in the Autobiographical Memoir prefixed to the edition of Newman's Letters by Anne Mozley (1891), it is correctly stated that "much as he owed to the Evangelical teaching, so it was he never had been a genuine Evangelical" (p. 122). Many changes had taken place in his views between his ordination on 13 June 1824 and the publication of the first of the *Tracts for the Times* in September 1833; it may be that the exact process of the changes will never be traced out. There can be no doubt as to the position Newman had reached, when the series of the *Tracts* began to appear. In a letter written on 31 August 1833 to his friend J. W. Bowden, he states quite clearly that "our objects are to rouse the clergy, to inculcate that Apostolical Succession, and to defend the Liturgy". The immediate occasion of the explosion was the decision of the political party in power to suppress a number of Anglican bishoprics in Ireland, a measure which appears in retrospect as one of the most reasonable measures ever put forward by a party in power. But to Newman, to whom by this time liberalism in any guise was anathema, as to his much more conservative friend John Keble, it appeared to be the beginning of national apostasy. Hence the appropriateness of the comment of James Mozley just about the time of the appearance of the first of the famous *Tracts* that "Newman is becoming perfectly ferocious in the cause".

It is to be noted that "apostolical succession" is not an Anglican phrase and does not appear in any Anglican official document. The Preface to the Anglican Ordinal does indeed declare that "from the Apostles' time there have been these Orders of Ministers in Christ's Church: Bishops, Priests and Deacons", and the rubrics to the services for the Making of Deacons and the Ordering of Priests instruct the preacher at these services to explain to the people "how necessary that Order is in the Church of Christ". But Newman and his friends seem to have been introducing into the Church of England a new and previously unknown concept of "necessity". Few, if any, of them would have denied that a devout nonconformist might be saved; but this they would have attributed to the uncovenanted mercies of God; no body without episcopacy, it was held, could lay any claim at all to the name and nature of a Church.

What then is the relation of the episcopal Church of England to other Churches? Some among Newman's followers found themselves much attracted by the "Branch theory" of the Church. The corporate unity of the Church has been broken, but its essential unity still remains. The Eastern Orthodox Churches, the great Western Church centred in Rome and the Anglican Churches have retained all the essentials of catholicity, including the episcopate, and should therefore recognize one another as being fully Churches, even though the way to full and visible unity may not as yet be open. This view never met with much favour in the Orthodox world, where the emphasis on absolute identity of doctrine made difficult any immediate rapprochement. The Roman Catholic administration, identifying as it did the Church of Christ with the Roman Catholic Church, could not recognize any other Christian body as being in reality a Church. The final blow was dealt to this theory by the unconditional condemnation of Anglican Orders pronounced by Leo XIII in the Bull *Apostolicae Curae* of 1896.

V. ECUMENICAL DEVELOPMENTS

Since 1833 there has been no one Anglican view of the necessity of episcopacy; various views have striven for the mastery within a co-existence of tensions. All Anglicans have accepted the fact of episcopacy; almost all have accepted it gladly, as a sign of the unity of the Church, as a safeguard against the tyranny of the individual parish priest and against eccentricity of doctrine beyond a certain point not too exactly defined.

The challenge which brought episcopacy once again into the forefront of Anglican controversy came once again from the far parts of the earth.

In 1919 four Churches in South India began the negotiations which led in 1947 to the formation of the Church of South India. It became clear from the start that the Anglican Church in India, from 1930 onwards a province independent of the control of the

Church of England, would not be interested in any scheme of union in which the historic episcopate was not included. It equally became apparent that the non-episcopal Churches would not accept any scheme of union which could make it appear that episcopacy had been imposed on them against their will by their Anglican colleagues. That in the end union came about was the result of a mysterious and laudable growing together to a common mind.

State episcopacy as practised up to the present day in England was abhorrent to the Free Churchmen. They were prepared to consider acceptance of the episcopate only when it came home to them that the Church of India, Burma and Ceylon had succeeded in recovering the true pastoral character of the episcopate to a far greater extent than either the Church of England or the Church of Rome. A Lord Bishop they would passionately repudiate; a Father in God might not be entirely unacceptable. Moreover, it had come home to these earnest Christians that in their own churches they had created a para-episcopate of Moderators, Superintendents and Presidents; the episcopate was not in practice as strange to them as they had thought. It was at this point that they began to be willing to say that in the past their ancestors for good reason had rejected a false episcopacy, but that a true episcopacy was something that they might be led to accept as expedient to the Church of South India in the twentieth century.

This once agreed, the question arose as to how non-episcopal churches could receive the episcopate. Controversy on this subject was long and apparently fruitless. Light dawned when all parties to the discussion came to agreement on the principle that the quality of a ministry is determined by the nature of the Church which it serves, but that the quality of a Church is not determined by the nature of the ministry which it possesses. A Church may have the most perfectly guaranteed episcopal succession; but if it departs from the truth of the gospel it is no longer a Church of Jesus Christ. A Church may have only rags and shreds of a succession; but, if it teaches the truth of the gospel, it is, however imperfectly, a Church of Jesus Christ. It was the clear statement of this principle which made it possible for sixty per cent of the bishops assembled in the Lambeth Conference of 1948 to vote in favour of immediate recognition of that Church of South India which had come into existence one year earlier. (This was not carried into effect until a later date.) It was the same principle which led the leaders of the Church of South India to accept the idea of a great act of unification of the separated Churches, but to reject any separate act of the reconciliation of the ministries; it was held that if Churches have been united, *a fortiori* their ministries have also been united.

This theological principle has not been accepted by all Churches engaged in the search for unity. In North India, in negotiations in which the Anglicans were engaged, there was a separate act of reconciliation of the ministries. Since all ministries in separation suffer from a measure of imperfection, all these ministries were to be offered up to God in the faith that he himself would give them back to the United Church in a new fullness of power and adequacy; the laying on of hands was to be taken as a sign of this faith and humble prayer.

A similar proposal was made in the plan to unite the Anglican and Methodist Churches in England. A considerable number of Anglicans had made it plain in advance that they could not conscientiously vote for a plan of union which contained such a ceremony for the unification of ministries, since the Methodists had declared that to them such a ceremony would add nothing to a ministry which they regarded as already having the fullness of ministry, and since it would be open to some Anglicans to regard the ceremony as being in fact episcopal ordination for those who had not received it. As had been foreseen, the plan failed to receive the required 75 per cent of Anglican votes, and is for the moment in abeyance, though the desire for union remains as strong as it ever was.

VI. CONCLUSION

In so short an article it has been necessary to be selective. But certain prevailing Anglican points of view may have become plain from this brief survey.

1. All Anglicans are agreed that the episcopate has been from the earliest times an element of the life of the Christian Church. If not instituted by Christ himself, it is at least consonant with what we know of the will of Christ for his Church.

2. Like all other forms of organization, episcopacy has often broken down and failed to fulfil its proper functions; but no more satisfactory form of church organization has ever yet been devised.

3. The office of bishop in the Church is primarily a spiritual function, concerned with the oversight of the flock after the pattern of Christ, who is himself the shepherd and overseer of our souls (1 Peter 2. 25).

4. Legal and hierarchical attributes which have become associated with the office of bishop are marginal, and in no way related to the essential functions which the bishop is there to perform in the Church of Christ.

5. A united Church should be richer than the churches in their separation. Anglicans have been privileged to retain in its fullness the treasure of the episcopate. It is unlikely therefore that they will be prepared to consider any scheme of union in which this treasure is not fully conserved.

6. But this high value set on the episcopate should not mislead the Church into denying the work of the Holy Spirit of God wherever it is found, even beyond the limits of the organized Churches which claim for themselves the name of Jesus Christ.

Piet Fransen

Some Aspects of the Dogmatization of Office

WHAT is this process that has come to be known as dogmatization? I use it here in the sense of an evolution in man's reflective awareness of Christian faith. This began as an imitation of the risen Lord, but gradually came to be expressed in a special language which in turn developed into doctrines that were to some extent binding in character.

Any study of this process obviously calls for historical and critical research,[1] but, in this short article in which I have to span almost two thousand years, I cannot even mention the necessary books and articles.[2] All that I can do is to throw light on some of the most important stages in this development. In this connection, it is important to point out that many aspects of the subject have never been studied in any detail, sometimes, as in the case of the ordinary priest in the patristic period and even later, because of lack of source material. Finally, I shall not be discussing the New Testament period, as this is dealt with elsewhere in this number.

My point of departure is the generally accepted view that the development of office in the first two centuries of the Church's

[1] See, for example, P. Fransen, "Unity and Confessional Statements. Historical and Theological Inquiry of R.C. Traditional Conceptions", in *Bijdragen* 33 (1972), pp. 2–38; this article includes a detailed bibliography concerning the questions discussed in the present essay.

[2] Good articles have been published in *Concilium* about this subject; see, for example, E. Schillebeeckx, ed., "Dogma and Pluralism", *Concilium*, Jan. 1970 (American Edn., Vol. 51) and K. Rahner, ed., "The Identity of the Priest", *Concilium*, March 1969 (American Edn., Vol. 43).

history was slow and uneven. This is one reason why it is difficult nowadays to accept the idea of a *ius divinum* in connection with office if this is not seen to be really part of a complex history.[3] I prefer the Tridentine formula *ordinatio divina* to *ius divinum*, even though the reasons for choosing this formula were different at the time of Trent from mine today.[4] My preference is based on the clarity with which the term expresses the fact that a human and often local choice goes hand in hand with a divine dispensation. Office in the Church may be accompanied by a saving act made by God in Christ, but it has to be expressed in social relationships which are historically conditioned. God's intention is also always expressed so much more richly in the Church's office than anything that we can make of it in any historical context.

Finally, it should also be borne in mind that the problem of dogmatization is above all a linguistic problem and that all use of language either includes or excludes certain forms of thought. What is more, language is closely related not only to thought but also to life itself—action is not simply expressed in speech, it *is* a speech. Both thought and speech also have a reciprocal effect on action.

How, then, can I be bold enough not only to interpret how thought and speech functioned at a certain period of history, but also to go further and to judge whether this marked a step forward or a step back? The criteria that the theologian can apply to this question are simply those of Scripture and the life of the Church and in this he is helped by the Spirit, who always

---

[3] In his article "Theologische kanttekeningen bij de huidige priestercrisis", in *Tijdschrift voor Theologie* 8 (1968), p. 415, E. Schillebeeckx referred to J. Neumann's "Erwägungen zur Revision des kirchlichen Gesetzbuches", in *Theologische Quartalschrift* 146 (1966), pp. 285-304. Neumann in turn had criticized K. Rahner's view that the *ius divinum* was "irreversible"; see K. Rahner, "Über den Begriff des 'ius divinum' im katholischen Verständnis", *Schriften zur Theologie*, V (Einsiedeln, 1962), pp. 249-77; see also Y. Congar, *Ministères et communion ecclésiale* (Paris, 1971), p. 32.
[4] P. Fransen, "Le Concile de Trente et le sacerdoce", *Le Prêtre, Foi et Contestation*, ed. A. Deschamps (Gembloux, 1970), pp. 106-42; Karl Lehmann, "Das dogmatische Problem des theologischen Ansatzes zum Verständnis des Amtpriestertums", in *Existenzprobleme des Priesters* (Munich, 1969), pp. 121-75, especially pp. 135-50.

guides the community of believers in assessing the value of these "external" criteria.

I. The Influence of the Old Testament

Anyone who examines the language of the first Christians is inevitably struck by their spontaneous and frequent quotations from the Old Testament, in contrast to modern theologians, who are far more cautious in their use of Old Testament concepts and symbols.

It is clear from the Council of Nicaea, for example, that non-Jewish converts only very hesitantly developed their own religious language, "Hellenizing" Christian dogma. Was there, on the other hand, ever a "Judaizing" of Christian thought about office in the Church? The New Testament authors clearly never gave office a "priestly" content, but, immediately after the apostolic era, authors such as Clement of Rome began to compare the apostles and their successors with the Jewish levitical priesthood. Throughout the patristic period this comparison was made more and more frequently in theology, the liturgy and even in legislation.[5]

Was this perhaps the beginning of an unjustified sacralization of office in the Church and of a return to a Jewish way of thinking? The priestly categories that were current at the time in the New Testament and even later were not applied to office in the Church and this may be because the words *kōhen*, *hiereus* and *sacerdos* had an unmistakable meaning in the linguistic usage of the time. The word "priest" could hardly be used in its abstract sense and detaching it from its traditional context was a necessary but slow process. It is always very difficult too for contemporaries to date the beginning of any process of development and to interpret its implications correctly.

The problem, however, goes deeper than this and confronts us with an important choice. There is always the possibility of a revival of Marcionitism if the influence of the Old Testament is rejected as a "Judaization" of office in the Church, thus placing the Old Testament and the history of the Jewish people outside

[5] See, for example, R Gryson, *Le prêtre selon saint Ambroise* (Louvain, 1968).

the main stream of revelation. But what precisely is "Judaization" in the formal sense and in what way did God come to the people gathered together within his Covenant? It is very difficult to answer this question, which is ultimately concerned with the difference between the substance of faith and its historical mode of expression.[6]

The Fathers of the Church were not, in my opinion, guilty of excessive "Judaization"—they were always aware that office was above all a "pneumatic" task in a sense that was unknown to the Jewish levites and priests and this awareness was moreover expressed in the everyday life of the Church. Both bishops and, as far as we know, priests were chosen by the people because of some "charismatic" gift interpreted in the widest sense.

The situation was, in my view, different in the Middle Ages, when Old Testament symbols, doctrines and even legal obligations such as the tithe were accepted freely and almost uncritically. The Old Testament priestly *ceremonalia* such as blood sacrifices and circumcision were excluded from Christian practice and it would seem that Christians thought of these as alien forms of ritual life. As we shall see later, because the charismatic character of office was obscured, there was no longer any way of counterbalancing this uncritical acceptance of the Old Testament.

II. THE INFLUENCE OF THE CONSTANTINIAN "ESTABLISHMENT"

The contemporary scapegoats in the question of the development of office in the Church are the Edict of Milan (313) and Constantine and his successors, who granted the bishops great privileges. Klauser suggested that this resulted in their being included within the state hierarchy and, although he has disputed Klauser's view, Jerg recognizes that it has become almost an *opinio communis*.[7] Furthermore, Klauser's position has been

---

[6] See E. Schillebeeckx's warning in his "Naar een katholiek gebruik van de hermeneutiek?" in H. van der Linde and H. A. M. Fiolet, eds., *Geloof bij het kenterend getij. Peilingen in een seculariserend Christendom* (Roermond and Maaseik, n.d.), pp. 78–116.

[7] T. Klauser, *Der Ursprung der bischöflichen Insignien und Ehrenrechte* (Bonner akademische Reden, 1) (Krefeld, 1949, ²1953); Ernst Jerg, *Vir venerabilis, Untersuchungen zur Titulatur der Bischöfe in den ausser-*

subtly modified in a number of monographs analysed by Jerg in his book and also by Gryson.

The *audientia episcopalis*, for example, was a kind of arbitration existing alongside the imperial jurisdiction, a court to which the Christian could appeal and which the bishop could refuse to attend. This function was regarded as a form of pastoral care at the time and less attention was given to the part played by the bishop in the city community, the only fairly autonomous governing body within the Empire. When the Empire collapsed, the bishop was thus in a position, as *pater civitatis*, to assume certain governing functions. In the West and especially in Rome, the State's *cura annonae* were gradually transferred to the Church. This originally pastoral care of the poor was the source of the Roman deacons' power and gave the bishop an increased social responsibility after the barbarian invasions.

It would be an exaggeration to claim that the bishops were included within the *cursus publicus*, which was notorious because of its cunning use of ranks and titles. One often has the impression that they belonged to the ranks of the *illustres* of the Curia, but, as Jerg has pointed out, the titles with which they were addressed in non-ecclesiastical letters and legal documents were used out of deference to their spiritual dignity.

This impression is strengthened by a study of the lives of some of the bishops. Ambrose, for example, was an official in the imperial court, but as soon as he was consecrated bishop, he became conscious of the new responsibility that he shared with his fellow bishops. Similarly, Augustine's attitude changed after his consecration. The monks and hermits in the Egyptian desert, on the other hand, were successful at least partly because they were protesting against the power of some of those holding office in the Church. The Church, however, assimilated this spirit of protest by emphasizing the charismatic and spiritual character of the bishop's function. In the East, this led to the practice of choosing bishops from among the monks. Gryson has, on the other hand,

---

kirchlichen Texten der Spätantike als Beitrag zur Deutung ihrer öffentlichen Stellung (Wiener Beiträge zur Theologie, 26) (Vienna, 1970); Jerg provides a detailed analysis of reactions to Klauser's argument and a full bibliography, pp. 11–71.

been able to find only one text in the writings of Ambrose referring to the ordinary priest, although it is known that Augustine
gathered his priests around him in a kind of monastic community, a practice which was probably followed by other bishops.

As van Roey has pointed out,[8] there were many abuses in practice, but the charismatic and evangelical aspects of the episcopate
were always stressed in theory in the patristic age, even though
there was a tendency to separate those holding office from the
laity in the Church, as the result of the "Judaizing" influence of
the Old Testament. Unconsciously and collectively, moreover,
certain choices were made, especially concerning originally pastoral social tasks, which ultimately led later to the integration of
office in the Church into the medieval feudal system. This is, of
course, another example of the tragic aspect of all human activity,
which can never completely escape the ambiguity of all man's
commitment.

It is also an example of the dangers involved in any process of
dogmatization, which takes place in a vacuum, whereas the
Church's office is above all rooted in a specific historical context,
in this case, that of the Byzantine and Holy Roman Empire. When
this historical situation developed and the emperors gained more
control over the Church, the Church was prevented by this very
process of dogmatization from dissociating itself quickly enough
from what was taking place. In other words, what was true in
A.D. 313 was probably not true at the time of Justinian or Charlemagne. The process of dogmatization is one of finding clear and
binding definitions, but not everything in this process can be
equally binding. Christians have, however, to gain a much deeper
understanding of the historical character of revelation before they
can appreciate this and this understanding was less accessible at
the beginning of the Middle Ages than ever before, with the
result that the process of dogmatization went hand in hand with
a process of strengthening the "establishment" and thus of limiting evangelical freedom.

---

[8] A. van Roey, "De derde man, Vragen aan de patrologie", *Aan mensen
gewaagd, Zicht op de identiteit van de priester*, ed. Joris Baers (Tielt and
Utrecht, 1972), pp. 67–80.

III. The "Res Publica Christiana"

The process of dogmatization was more obvious during this period, which lasted some nine centuries, with the result that I shall have to generalize to some extent. Rome kept in touch with the East after the barbarian invasions, but central and northern Europe became a complex world of tribal and later dynastic bonds of feudal loyalty and submission, subject to the capricious interplay of alliances, marriages and hereditary succession.

Bishops, abbots and chapters were all included in the complicated economic, social and political structure of the Holy Roman Empire. Even as late as the French Revolution, bishops had the status of princes of the Church, as opposed to the *principes saeculares*, with the result that only the sons of noblemen were as a rule accepted as bishops. The ordinary priests were sent to churches and chapels with benefices endowed by princes of the Church or by secular princes, so that their bond with the bishop or the local church, which had hitherto formed so important a part of their vocation, became many different bonds of feudal loyalty to many different masters. Their functions became more and more exclusively cultic, partly because the monks and mendicant friars had already begun to perform most of the apostolic tasks.

The clerical order had a higher status than the laity in a society of orders and, by the eighth century, this conviction had been given a theological foundation. But, according to Congar,[9] the roots of an even more serious problem were to be found at the level of the pope and the hierarchy. From the time of Charlemagne onwards, the Church became more and more subject to the secular power, culminating in the conflict between pope and emperor in the eleventh and twelfth centuries about the right to investiture. Basically, it was a struggle for privilege, financial rights and above all for power—the first written works about the hierarchy were entitled *De potestate ecclesiastica*—and this had a

[9] Y.-M. Congar, "The Historical Development of Authority in the Church", *Problems of Authority*, ed. John M. Todd (London and Baltimore, 1962), pp. 119–50.

very damaging effect on the charismatic view of the episcopate and on the priesthood in general.[10]

This historical development was reflected quite closely in a parallel development in theology as an aspect of the process of dogmatization. The most dangerous consequence of this was the division of the one office into the two powers of ordination and government.[11] Basing their reasoning on the Ambrosiaster and especially on Jerome, theologians saw no difference between bishop and priest apart from the former's power of government. The power of ordination was determined by another *potestas*, the power to change the bread and wine into the body and blood of the Lord, the miracle that obsessed medieval man, together with the priest's power to intercede "for the living and the dead". For two or three centuries, there was no agreement about the sacrament of penance, until Thomas Aquinas produced good arguments for linking the power of absolution with that of ordination. This whole process of dogmatization was completed at the Councils of Florence and Trent in a general acceptance of this cultic view as a doctrine of the Church. All the same, this diminution of the idea of office in the Church was not accepted by everyone and especially not by the canon lawyers, who maintained contact with the earlier theology of previous councils and of the Church Fathers.

IV. The Process of "Dis-establishment"

All with all, the pattern of development which followed this era of growing "establishment" was one of extremely slow "dis-establishment". In very broad outline, this began with radical protest against clericalization in the Church from the fourteenth century onwards—from Ockham and Marsilius of Padua, Wyclif and Huss to the Reformation and then from the Enlightenment to the modern phenomenon of anticlericalism. It is hardly possible to claim that this protest, unchanging in character despite

---

[10] See G. Pfeilschifter, ed., *Acta Reformationis Catholicae Ecclesiam Germaniae concernentia saeculi XVI*; the fifth and penultimate volume has just appeared, Band IV/2 (Regensburg, 1959–1971).

[11] J. Ratzinger, "Opfer, Sakrament und Priestertum in der Entwicklung der Kirche", *Catholica* 26 (1972), pp. 108–25.

changing circumstances and ever-increasing intensity, has not been sustained by a genuine religious concern.

The Church has reacted very slowly indeed to this protest. It is clear from the development from the Council of Trent via the First Vatican Council to the Second that the Church has moved from a paralysing connection with the State to an almost complete spiritual freedom. The State too has evolved from an enlightened despotism to a secularization that makes anticlericalism look very archaic.

Much more is known about the ordinary priest in this period. His range of possible tasks increased and the reforms of the Council of Trent with regard to the priesthood were very influential, especially in the provision of seminary training. Following Trent, the dogmatization of the idea of the priesthood was furthered by an increasing emphasis on spirituality. Two movements have played an all important part in the spiritual and intellectual formation of the priest—the French school of Bérulle, de Condren and Olier, which led directly to the Sulpician seminaries, whose influence spread to Canada and the United States and then to the developing countries, and a second movement in Belgium and France which concentrated on training the diocesan clergy. Both movements based their activity on dogmatic considerations and, together with the renewal movements that have emerged as a result of Vatican II, they have provided priests with a rich and inspiring preparation.

Is it also possible to detect the influence of these movements on the process of dogmatization? It was obviously almost inevitable that the rediscovery of a much richer and more flexible tradition should cause great tension between the familiar ideology of the Church of the past and the fervent hopes of the Church of the present and the future released by Vatican II. Less positive features were discovered in the earlier traditions of spirituality. The excessive emphasis placed in the West on the priest's sharing in the one priesthood of Christ was compared unfavourably with the Eastern view that the priest is borne up by the Spirit and makes Christ's work present in the Church. The traditionally ontological approach of the Church to the sacramental sign was seen as the cause of possible "metaphysical" clericalism and of isolating the priest from and placing him above the lay people of

God. The Tridentine decision to set up seminaries for the separate spiritual and theological training of priests away from the world led to positive achievements, but, like all human action, it also resulted in ambiguity—it meant that the priest became alienated from the rapidly developing world of technological progress.

CONCLUSION

It is quite clear that the process of dogmatization has in no sense ceased or reached fruition. Any attempt to reformulate the Church's teaching about the priesthood must be preceded by at least an elementary historical investigation of office in the Church —history opens us to the *kairos* of the present. In the words of C. S. Lewis, "the unhistorical are usually, without knowing it, enslaved to a fairly recent past".[12]

[12] C. S. Lewis, *De Destructione Temporum*, Inaugural Lecture (Cambridge, 1954), reprinted in *They Asked for a Paper* (London, 1962), p. 23.

Translated by David Smith

PART II
BULLETIN

Joan Brothers

Women in Ecclesial Office

INTEREST in the ordination of women is distinctly a minority taste. Relatively few people can approach the question with even a degree of objectivity. Even those who are generally in favour of basic changes in the structures of the Church seem to find it hard to take this issue seriously. Either it is out of the question, or it is a matter which is not worth treating seriously; to most it is something unimportant, even silly or amusing. Apart from the work of specialized study groups or conferences on the subject, especially those set up by the World Council of Churches, literature on the subject comes largely from women themselves. Indeed, it is notable that even comments from radical critics like Ivan Illich[1] on the need to rethink the nature of the priesthood omit from their discussions the question of the ordination of women.

Yet there are some Christian denominations which have found it possible to admit women to the ministry. (What they do with them afterwards is another matter, and this is discussed later.) The Congregationalists have admitted women to the ministry for a number of years, and the Universalist Church of America has had women ministers from very early days. Since the war a number of Reformed churches have admitted women to the pastorate; in fact, about seventy-two of the constituent churches of the World Council of Churches now ordain women.[2] (In the

[1] "The Vanishing Clergyman", in *Celebration of Awareness* (London, 1971).
[2] *What is Ordination Coming to?* Report of a consultation on the ordina-

United States a woman—Sally Preisand—is studying for the rabbinate within Reform Judaism, though there are problems of her being recognized as a rabbi by a congregation.)

In a number of churches the matter is much discussed. In the Roman Catholic Church those attending conferences on religious themes have frequently been disconcerted to discover that there are strong pressures on the part of some participants to accept motions proposing the ordination of women; the majority is still quite good at resisting such pressures.

The question of the admission of women to ecclesial offices is currently very important for those Christian churches which do not yet admit women to these offices, for two reasons.

(1) First of all, there are women who believe that they have a vocation to the ministry. Those women who believe that they may be able to serve the Christian community in this way may be a very small number, but their convictions are plainly sincere and strongly held, and as such deserve more than the patronizing treatment they currently receive.

(2) Secondly, as Mary Daly has pointed out in her book *The Church and the Second Sex*, in this issue of the admission of women to the priesthood, "the whole problem of the situation of women in the Church is reflected, symbolized and crystallized. Indeed, it is evident to anyone who has repeatedly engaged in discussions of the subject that this can serve as a touchstone of attitudes concerning women and the man-woman relationship."[3] The assumptions underlying this point cannot be sufficiently emphasized. They were raised a few years ago by Lukas Vischer of the World Council of Churches in the question: "Does the Church adequately reflect the great truth that *in Christ there is neither male nor female*? Does the Order of the Church adequately express this truth?"[4]

For those who have not been following the debate, let us now

---

tion of women, edited by Brigalia Bam (World Council of Churches, 1971). See also "Woman's Place in the Ministry of Non-Catholic Christian Churches", *Concilium*, April 1968 (American Edn., Vol. 34).

[3] New York, 1968, p. 154.

[4] "The Ordination of Women", in *Concerning the Ordination of Women* (World Council of Churches, 1964).

ask: *What are the main trends in the literature which is generally available?*

I. WOMEN IN CHURCH AND SOCIETY

1. *Societal Changes*

First, I think it is reasonable to suggest that the pastoral content and purport of recent writings on women in the Church will be better appreciated if seen against the background of contemporary feminist writings. It must be stressed that by no means all those interested in the ordination accept the position of women's liberation movements. On the one hand, some write from a much more conventional perspective; and on the other hand, much work predates the current wave of writings on the subject of women. And within the women's liberation groups religious questions do not generally take on much interest except in negative terms, in that a number of writers—Eva Figes, for example[5]—are highly critical of the part played by the Church in suppressing women. But without some knowledge of what is being currently written, read, and, above all, *felt* on this general question, it will be hard to appreciate what is happening in specifically religious contexts. (It may be *possible* to estimate the political significance of Black Power at the grass roots level without reading people like Frantz Fanon and Eldridge Cleaver; whether to try to do so is *sensible* is another matter.) Kate Miller's *Sexual Politics* is an obvious starting-point.[6] In *Woman's Estate*, Juliet Mitchell has brought together a great deal of material, including her own seminal statement of the socialist feminist position.[7] A more idiosyncratic view which is being widely read at the present time is Germaine Greer's *The Female Eunuch*.[8]

The significance of these writings as social documents cannot be sufficiently underlined. First of all, though those who write and speak in public on such issues are in the minority, they are to some degree articulating the growing sense of frustration that is experienced by an increasing number of women as they realize that societal permissiveness in relation to their personal and pro-

---

[5] *Patriarchal Attitudes* (London, 1970). See also Sarah Doely, *Women's Liberation and the Church* (New York, 1970).
[6] New York, 1970.   [7] London, 1971.   [8] London, 1970.

fessional needs usually means that they are allowed to bear the tensions of additional roles and responsibilities in employment while being freed from notably few of the traditional expectations relating to femininity.

Secondly, such writings provide an ideology for women which enables them to interpret some of the economic, political and social sources of their status and lack of power in contemporary industrialized societies.

If the question of the admission of women to the priesthood and diaconate is seen against the background of irreversible and increasingly international trends regarding the position of women, it cannot be dismissed as the goal of the eccentric view but has to be seen as representing the inevitable outcome of wider socio-economic changes. The general desire to abolish discrimination against women has its outcome in religious as well as other spheres.

2. *Church Renewal*

Those who seek ordination, male or female, in any church, are in the minority, and it is essential to see the question of ordination as one part—though of very considerable symbolic significance—of the wider desire of women to participate on equal terms in the life of the Church. St Joan's International Alliance, founded as early as 1911, has been unfailing in its efforts to draw attention to discrimination against women in the Church, and has for some time asked that the priesthood be extended to women. A number of study groups in various countries are considering the position of women in the Church, some with precise aims in relation to women's functions, others seeing their position as illustrative of the general need for renewal. Notable amongst such groups is the Dutch "Samenwerking man en vrouw in de kerk", which has done a great deal to promote discussions and publications on the ordination of women. The international group "Femmes et Hommes dans l'Eglise" has published interventions made by the bishops during the 1971 Synod in Rome relating to women, and in particular to conferring the ministry on women.

In spite of the resolutions adopted by various congresses and conferences (for instance, the fifth resolution of the third World

Congress of the Lay Apostolate in 1967, and the proposition accepted at the international theological congress held under the auspices of *Concilium* in 1970) and other attempts to alter the position of women in the formal structures of the Church, liturgical reforms have still not advanced very far in relation to women.[9] Similarly, their representation in the Church's official structures is still very slight.[10]

Impatient with the tepid conclusions often reached that the question needs further investigation, there have been a number of appeals from different quarters for a Commission to be set up as quickly as possible to study the question of the admission of women to the priesthood and diaconate.

3. *The Religious Life*

It should also be added that much of the current literature about women in the religious life is relevant to the wider question of the status of women in the Church, reflecting as it does the need to cede more autonomy for their own lives to women's congregations. That not all frustration in relation to the position and status of women in religion can be dealt with effectively within and by the system is instanced in the fact that among women currently leaving the religious life are those who, far from feeling that they are not suited to the religious state, consider that they cannot realize their individual vocations within religious communities as they are now constituted, and whose efforts to change those communities have been unsuccessful not because of the wishes of the members of the immediate community itself but because of clashes with church rules or authorities.

II. Theological Discussions

The intensive theological discussions which preceded the ordination in some Christian denominations have been generally available for some time. Such discussions have emphasized the need to interpret scriptural evidence in the light of contemporary

[9] See René Van Eyden, "The Place of Women in Liturgical Functions", *Concilium*, Feb. 1972 (American Edn., Vol. 72), especially pp. 76–8.
[10] See the Special Note Number 21 produced by *Pro Mundi Vita*, "Men and Women in Partnership in the Church and in Society".

exegetical research,[11] and theological traditions in relation to particular cultural conditions. Nor need such steps necessarily be seen as an obstacle to ecumenism. A few years ago André Dumas, at the end of a very clear review of evidence from the New Testament and systematic theology, urged that the recognition of women as ministers should be interpreted by the churches together "not as an influence of secularism, but as a fruit of biblical and liturgical renewal".[12] An admirable summary of the position obtaining in the Christian churches, including the Orthodox, has been given by Madeleine Barot.[13]

Not all those churches which have given serious attention to debating the theological implications of the ordination of women have taken the step of admitting them to the ministry. Thus, the Anglican commission admits women to the office of deaconess (this order was revived in 1862), but the step of ordaining women has not been generally accepted.[14] It is significant that at the Lambeth Conference of 1968 there were observers from other churches who said that the ordination of women "would create a further obstacle to unity in practice, *even if no certain theological arguments stood in the way*"[15] (my italics). At the plenary session it was stated that the reasons against the ordination of women were at present inconclusive. The debate still continues, and in 1971 two Anglican women were ordained in Hong Kong.[16]

Amongst Roman Catholics there now seems to be some measure of agreement that the objections to the ordination of women are on the pastoral, cultural or emotional rather than the theological level. So, for instance, René Van Eyden cites the research of Haye van der Meer's "Subjectum ordinationis est mas": "It was not his intention to give proof for or against, but only to

[11] See, for instance, Krister Stendhal, *The Bible and the Role of Women* (Philadelphia, 1966); and Marga Bührig, "The Question of the Ordination of Women in the Light of Some New Testament Texts", in *Concerning the Ordination of Women, op. cit.,* pp. 41–5.
[12] "Biblical Anthropology and the Participation of Women in the Ministry of the Church", in *Concerning the Ordination of Women, op. cit.,* p. 40.
[13] "Dialogue des Eglises", *Echanges,* 96 (May 1970), pp. 20–6.
[14] See M. E. Thrall, *The Ordination of Women* (London, 1958); and the Report of a Commission appointed by the Archbishops of Canterbury and York, *Women and Holy Orders* (London, 1966).
[15] John Coventry, "Lambeth 1968", *One in Christ,* V, 1 (1969), p. 15.
[16] See *The Time is Now,* Anglican Consultative Council, First Meeting (London, 1971).

consider critically the conclusiveness of current arguments against women in the ministry. The result was surprising: none of the arguments which are put forward proved to be tenable. His conclusion is therefore that it is by no means an established fact that ordination is *iure divino* inaccessible to women."[17]

Both René Van Eyden and Yvonne Pelle-Douël[18] make mention of Cardinal Daniélou's recent comment that there is no theological or structural obstacle to the ordination of women. (He had earlier written: "I would say that I see none of the duties of the minor orders which, so far as the female aspect of them is concerned, cannot be, and in fact have not been, undertaken by a woman."[19])

Other Roman Catholic writers who have recently contributed on the subject include Sister Vincent Emmanuel Hannon[20] and Mary Daly.[21] The latter cites Hans Küng's comments that there are neither dogmatic nor biblical reasons against the ordination of women, the factors to be considered being psychological and sociological. Daly's pungent analysis stresses that since cultural conditions have *already* changed in relation to women the situation within the Catholic Church is anachronistic. She is thus voicing the fear shared by many that the new grounds on which women are held to be excluded from the ministry may prove as resistant to change as theological objections were in the past.

This current shift of emphasis can be interpreted as the replacement of the conservatism of the theological élite by the sociologically observed conservatism of the masses. In most social systems changes are commonly resisted by the appeal: "It's not *me* that's objecting, it's society at large."

If there seems to be some measure of agreement that there are no theological or scriptural arguments of any substance[22] and an

[17] "Women Ministers in the Catholic Church", *Sisters Today*, 40, No. 4 (Dec. 1968), pp. 214-15. See H. van der Meer, *Priestertum der Frau?*, Coll. Quaestiones Disputatae 42 (Freiburg, 1969).
[18] Interview, *Informations Catholiques Internationales*, No. 400 (15 Jan. 1972), p. 22.
[19] *The Ministry of Women in the Early Church* (London, 1961), p. 30.
[20] *The Question of Women and the Priesthood* (London, 1967).
[21] *Op. cit.*
[22] See Eric Doyle, "God and the Feminine", *The Clergy Review*, LVI, 11 (Nov. 1971), p. 877; and Sister Margaret Rowe, "Women in the Church", *Herder Correspondence*, VI, 10 (Oct. 1969), pp. 291-8.

increasing amount of literature urging that the traditional evidence has to be interpreted in the light of earlier cultural conditions, what objections can currently be made within the Roman Catholic church to the admission of women to the priesthood and diaconate?

III. Roman Catholic Objections to Women in Office

1. Clerical Roles and Functions

A major set of objections to the ordination of women rest upon the alleged inability of women to perform traditional clerical roles. People are accustomed, it is said, to men performing liturgical functions and would not easily accept women doing so. Since there is no experience of this role reversal in the Roman Catholic Church, we cannot say with any degree of assurance that congregations would react in this way. Other churches have found it possible to participate in the liturgy celebrated by women. Like liturgical changes which seem startling in theory and obvious enough when realized, the experience of being present at a service offered by a woman, or indeed a Mass celebrated by one, as is possible in the Swedish Lutheran Church, can seem very matter of fact. In many denominations, women have preached for some time, and many lay Catholics might feel that the key question relates to the capability of the preacher rather than to the sex. Moreover, there are now pastoral situations in the Church (for instance, Brazil, Uganda, Kinshasa City) where nuns already undertake many liturgical functions, including baptism, marriage, funerals and leading liturgical assemblies.[23]

Characteristic of the more emotional objections which are raised in relation to clerical roles and functions is that people would not like to confess their sins to women. Such an objection ignores the fact that the practice of private confession is declining in many areas. More fundamentally, it illustrates how opponents commonly select one priestly function alone. There is a good deal more to the pastorate than hearing confessions, and there is no reason to suppose that women would prove less capable of

[23] See *Pro Mundi Vita*, Note Number 21, *op. cit.*

visiting homes and hospitals, acting as chaplains to industrial missions, universities or hospitals (where, after all, women are a substantial part of the work force or population) or other specialized ministries than men. Indeed, many religious or lay women already carry out identical pastoral roles.

Tine Govaart-Halkes, in a contribution to the World Council of Churches Consultation on the ordination of women held in Switzerland in 1970, comments on the movement on the part of some Roman Catholic theologians towards seeing the objections as being non-theological. Her point in this context is crucial: instead of regarding prejudice against women as immovable, the problem is to educate congregations: "Perhaps one can find new forms, forms of ministry in which everything is new, including the way in which the male minister is to function so that men and women work it out together—not compelling or forcing parishes to accept such ministries, but hoping, praying and believing in the Spirit that flexibility can develop in men and women so that they may gradually accept such new ministries."[24]

If women are not ideally suited to current clerical roles or lifestyles, this may tell us more than we know about those roles and patterns of behaviour. Yvonne Pelle-Douël has put her finger on the problem when she remarks that women are not asking to be allowed to don the old soutanes which men no longer want.[25]

The emphasis currently placed by many theologians—Gregory Baum, for instance—upon the priestly role of service rather than that of offering sacrifice has been reflected in writings on women. This point is put very clearly in *Diakonos* (the bulletin, compiled by Mary Schaefer, of a Canadian group seeking the restoration of the office of deaconess) after a meeting in 1971 with the Canadian bishops to discuss the status of women: "The whole emphasis in ministry today is on service, and since priesthood has lost its prestige and has sometimes become a humiliation (and thus so much more Christ-like), we can only see the ministry as cleansed of its aspirations for power. Nor, most assuredly, do we want to be men! We do not want to become part of that pursuit for power or prestige or dominance which is too often part of

---

[24] In *What is Ordination Coming to?*, cit. sup., p. 32.
[25] *Cit. sup.*, cf. Elisabeth Gössmann, "Women as Priests?", *Concilium*, April 1968 (American Edn., Vol. 34).

the male behaviour pattern. We only ask that women be trusted to develop ordained ministry in their own distinctive ways."[26]

Perhaps one of the greatest structural obstacles to the admission of women to the priesthood and diaconate lies in an unwillingness to rethink the whole training and deployment of the clergy. In fact, the current problems of recruiting and retaining clerical professionals in all denominations are likely to produce far more radical consequences in this direction than any amount of previous flirtations with "reforms" in seminary orientation and deployment of the clergy.

2. After Ordination

Another set of objections to the ordination of women can be raised on the grounds that they will find it difficult to be appointed to congregations afterwards. Naturally, any changes in the laws and rules of a church in relation to the admission of women to ecclesial orders cannot guarantee what will happen to them afterwards. One of the major problems about legislation enabling a minority to take up particular professional tasks is that it can only act negatively in that those who actively discriminate become subject to sanctions. Changing popular attitudes is far harder.

Thus, in many instances, those women who have been admitted to the ministry have experienced painful situations. Moreover, there can be serious upheavals in the church in question following ordination, as is instanced in the Lutheran Church in Sweden which admitted women to the ministry in 1960. This has been given as one objection of a serious nature by a recent Anglican writer.[27] A study carried out by Elsie Gibson of ministers of twenty churches, showed that they experienced considerable discrimination from men colleagues.[28] While this may deter some women, the fact that such problems arise cannot, however, be used as a general argument against ordination. There are

[26] No. 5 (May 1971), pp. 7–8. See also E. R. Hudson, "Women and the Diaconate", *The Clergy Review*, LVI, 11 (Nov. 1971).

[27] Sue Flockton, *Why Not Ordain Women?* The Church Union (London, n.d.).

[28] *When the Minister is a Woman* (New York, 1970). See also, R. W. Henderson, "Reflections on the Ordination of Women", *Study Encounter*, VII, 1 (1971).

some congregations which have accepted women, and, as has been said before, there is no reason why their ministry should be confined only to local congregations. Many specialized ministries now exist in the Church, and there are calls on all sides for more.

It can be argued that the failure to amend canon law only perpetuates the existing sense of strangeness of the situation and reinforces the unconscious fears that some sections of the population apparently experience over women taking on unfamiliar roles and functions. With the exception of the U.S.S.R. where three-quarters of the medical profession are women, women doctors often experience discrimination, being relegated perhaps to particular branches of medicine or to lower paid sections of the profession; but no one any longer thinks that they should not be admitted to the profession simply because hostile or suspicious attitudes are still held by some male members of the profession and sections of the public alike. The problem is to change existing discriminatory attitudes, not to elevate them into a moral position.

3. Women as a "Special Case"

Probably the most ominous obstacle to the ordination of women lies in the vast amount of literature which reflects and continually reinforces the feeling that women have a special place in the Church as in life in general.[29] The Anglican theologian E. L. Mascall is amongst those who have used as an argument against the ordination of women that the difference in the sexes is reflected in the different roles they play in the work of redemption.[30] Notions concerning the special status or dignity of women have always been found by those within feminist movements to be a major obstacle to change. The resentment towards this emotional patterning of sex roles is only part of a general movement in the world against special categories. (One can instance the growing dislike amongst some students of élitist educational programmes

---

[29] The literature in this area is too vast to list. An example can be found in Teilhard de Chardin's poem, *The Eternal Feminine*; see H. de Lubac, *The Eternal Feminine. A Study on the Poem by Teilhard de Chardin* (London, 1971).

[30] "The Ministry of Women", *Theology*, LVII, 413 (Nov. 1954).

which concentrate upon the needs of the intellectually able, ignoring the social predefinitions which have made them such; or the awareness of racial prejudice in its more subtle forms, reinforcing the "distinctive" characteristics of a particular group.)

Seen sociologically, one of the ways in which change is characteristically avoided in any social system is by the creation of an ideology which legitimates the existing situation. We are all aware of how this is done in terms which are immediately discernible as damaging to a group. (For instance, the inadequate education of a section of children being justified on the grounds that the group in question is incapable of responding to the more prestigious offers made to other groups.) But an apparently *positive* image can also militate far more powerfully and subtly against change. In religious terms, the images of women as, for instance, maternal figures, ignoring the fact that this experience will not be possible for many women irrespective of their choice, and increasingly rejected by others, operates in this way; or seeing women as creatures of emotion or impulse, ignoring the conditions which have hitherto suppressed and punished the development of other characteristics or described them as masculine. In the professions, women are often judged according to special criteria relating to such images—does she look attractive *as well as* being a good doctor, does she cook well *as well as* being a good teacher?—rather than according to the conventional professional judgments relating to skill, knowledge and so on.

A recent writer on the Church's attitude towards women has this to say: "Motherhood and virginity have been extolled, and they are good values to have, but they are only facets of a woman's life, high in a hierarchy of values, but still only part of the expression of the person, not its totality. The primary factor which gives women their dignity is that they were created by the Father and redeemed by Christ, just as man has his essential dignity from this fact rather than because he is a father or a monk."[31] She goes on to say this about the ordination of women in the Roman Catholic Church: "The idea of a woman occupying a place of authority in the Church, with power over men, has been

[31] Patricia Worden, "Women in the Church", *The Newman*, IV, 4 (1969), p. 181.

strongly rejected. But this rejection rests on a misconception of the nature of the priesthood and the role of the priest in the Christian community as well as on a misunderstanding of the nature of authority. True authority is creative, as the origin of the word suggests: 'authority' meant as power is a corruption of the meaning. When our ideas on authority are clarified the way to a better understanding of the priesthood will be open. Once this is formulated it will be easier for the Church to accept the idea, intellectually and emotionally, that women as well as men can be presbyters, presiding at the liturgy, sharing in the prophetic function in preaching and serving as the focal point of unity for the local community, which today is the parish."[32]

As Catholics we have traditionally shared a symbolic world relating to Christ, the priesthood and the Church. In that shared construction of reality the images we had for the priesthood related to leadership and authority, symbols which in an earlier age were inevitably associated with masculine roles and functions. Clearly the need to sustain a celibate clergy contributed to the development of an ideological system in which men and women had distinctive and discrete destinies and purposes. Now this symbolic world is changing in two directions. On the one hand, for some the meaning they now attach to the priesthood is in terms of service to the community. On the other hand, as people become increasingly aware that differences between men and women relate more to the social patterning of roles in particular cultures rather than to innate, foreordained differences, the old symbolic order seems increasingly strange and unrelated to the new pastoral situations they encounter.

In the Church we are currently in the general process of developing new symbols to interpret our changing societal experiences. The difficulties that some find in envisaging women as priests seems to exemplify the general problems of developing language, symbols and images to describe, interpret and give meaning and purpose to the world we inhabit.

The admission of women to the priesthood and diaconate is not likely to produce an enormous spate of applications. There are some women who are preparing themselves for the priest-

[32] *Ibid.*, p. 182.

hood, confident that the Church will change its position. Some more will be drawn later on. But the numbers may well always be small. The formal removal of legal obstacles to the ordination of women will not remove the social or psychological obstacles but it would mean that those who were willing to battle with them would at least be able to do so. Such a decision would probably not have great statistical consequences, at least in the immediate future. But it would perhaps have unintended social and religious consequences, amongst which might be the renewal of the pledge to a more open Christian community.

PART III
DOCUMENTATION
CONCILIUM

Jan Kerkhofs

Office in the Church:
A Review and Comparison of
Recent Surveys among Priests

BETWEEN 1967 and 1971 several sociological surveys were carried out in a number of countries in the West and in certain parts of the Third World in order to gain information about the priest. The initiative was taken firstly by bishops' conferences and secondly by groups of priests, research institutes or pastoral centres. Some surveys (Zaïre, for example), which were not scientifically conducted, none the less reflect the situation in the country just as well as the scientific surveys carried out in the West, where financial resources and technical know-how are available and where there is a different attitude to surveys.

There was also a wide range of motives, from the desire to be as well informed as possible to the hope that the results would confirm or contradict certain pastoral—or political—choices. Some surveys (the Netherlands, Germany, Switzerland) were conducted with national synods or pastoral councils, others (U.S.A., Canada) with the Roman Synod of 1971 in mind. In the case of Spain, for instance, the survey was one element in a concerted attempt to throw light on the tensions existing within the clergy and between the clergy and the hierarchy.

It is hardly surprising that so many surveys have been carried out. There is, after all, a grave crisis in the priesthood.[1] Several

[1] See M. Kaufmann, "Regard statistique sur les prêtres qui quittent le ministère", in *Social Compass* 4 (1970), p. 499; E. Schallert, *The Catholic Priesthood, 1965–1971. An Analysis of the Principal Scientific Studies on the Condition of the Priesthood in the U.S. and Canada* (University of San Francisco, 1971); C. J. Caviglia, *The Catholic Priesthood in the*

of the documents of Vatican II, moreover, point to the value of
sociology in the study of pastoral problems and in "reading the
signs of the times". It is well to recognize that sociology can
only play a limited part in this and that other disciplines have
an equally important contribution to make. The considered and
always provisional answers to these problems will eventually be
reached through collaboration between experts in all these fields.
Despite the frequent demand that the Church leaders should
base their policy and decisions on scientific research, it is clear
that their attitude should not always be governed, for example,
by the results of public opinion polls among the clergy and laity.
They may have good reasons for going against public opinion in
the Church. On the other hand, however, they may form an exclusive "in-group" because of their age, education and the way
they were appointed and therefore have a "collective consciousness".[2] There have also been times when groups or individuals
(for example, the emperor) within the Church have had to liber-
ate the leaders (even the pope) from one-sided attitudes. We may
conclude by saying firstly that a relative value should be accorded
to all sociological surveys and secondly that we should be critical
in our attitude towards those who give *too* relative a value to all
scientific investigation of social religious problems.

In such a short article, all that I can do is to describe briefly the
scope and results of the most important surveys carried out and
make a few comments on each. In reading these comments, five
factors should be borne in mind: the great differences between
(1) the social situations of the groups surveyed (for example, the
Netherlands and Bolivia) and (2) the methods used in each survey; (3) volunteers from socially élite groups took part in most

U.S., 1965-1970. A Statistical Study of Growth Loss (ibid., 1971);
"The Priest of 1971 in Search of his Identity. Special Note 18", *Pro
Mundi Vita* (1971); L. Schneider and L. Zurcher, "Toward Understanding
the Catholic Crisis: Observations on Dissident Priests in Texas", *Journal
for the Scientific Study of Religion* 9 (Notre Dame, Indiana, 1970),
pp. 197–207.
  [2] In addition to the works of Peter Berger, Thomas Luckmann and
others, see Henri Desroche, *Sociologies religieuses* (Paris, 1968); J. Séguy,
"Sociologie de la connaissance et sociologie des religions", *Archives de
Sociologie des Religions* 15, 30 (1970), pp. 91–108. See also, for example,
the Spanish episcopate up to 1967–1968; a psychological study of the Irish
in-group in Church leadership would also be interesting.

of the surveys; (4) few or no comparisons have so far been made with surveys carried out in parallel groups (such as the Protestant clergy, doctors, lawyers, teachers) and finally (5) there are very few parallel psychological studies in existence.

EUROPE

The Netherlands

Dutch sociologists were the first to conduct a scientific study of the priest on a national scale. One of the tasks of the Catholic Institute of Sociology (KASKI) at The Hague is to keep accurate and up-to-date statistical information about ordinations and joining and leaving the religious and secular priesthood. The most important of all the other surveys carried out elsewhere in the Netherlands, however, was that conducted by the Institute of Applied Sociology at Nijmegen University at the request of the Dutch bishops into "priestly celibacy in a changing Church".[3] This inquiry revealed a clear correlation between the views about the priesthood held by the religious and secular priests and the students who were interviewed and their image of the Church. The principle of inter-disciplinary collaboration was also put into practice, sociologists, psychologists, theologians and a representative of the episcopate working together as a team in close contact with the leaders of the Church. The team's aim from the outset was to publish the results and, with the help of a team of theologians, to try to find solutions to the problems that emerged. The results of this inquiry have been confirmed to some extent by other surveys among both Catholic and Protestant clergy engaged in pastoral work and among the laity.[4] A special survey has also been carried out among parents (1,745 couples), ascertaining their views about office in the Church, including the religious.[5]

---

[3] *Ambtscelibaat in een veranderenke Kerk*, published by the Pastoral Institute of the Dutch Church, Rotterdam, and by Katholiek Archief (Amersfoort, 1969).

[4] J. B. Fabery, de Jonge, W. Berger, C. Boekestijn and I. M. van der Lans, *Zielzorger in Nederland, positie, taak en ambt van de pastor* (Meppel, 1968).

[5] *De Leek over het Ambt (Beeld en attraktiviteit van het ambt van priester, broeder en zuster)* (Instituut voor Toegepaste Sociologie, in cooperation with KASKI, 1967).

Germany

The German *Institut für Demoskopie*, based at Allenbach, was recently commissioned by the German bishops to carry out a survey among all Catholics above the age of sixteen to obtain information about their views concerning faith and the Church. The institute completed the first part of this inquiry in 1970, obtaining written replies from four and a half million Catholics out of a total of twenty-one million questionnaires sent out. This written inquiry was followed by an oral survey among a representative sample of 4,000 Catholics in 1970 and, at the beginning of 1971, a second written inquiry was conducted among all the secular and religious clergy, obtaining a 76.5% response. The final results of this very recent investigation have not yet been fully assessed,[6] but it is already possible to compare the views of lay Catholics varying between fully and non-practising and those of the clergy. What is more, the survey among the priests is less directly concerned with celibacy than the Dutch inquiry. The basic patterns of thought among German Catholics are, however, very similar to those revealed in the Dutch survey. The polarization between the two images of the Church—on the one hand a sacral image and on the other a desacralized image— is less sharp than in the Netherlands, but it is none the less present.

Several factors are clear from the material already published. (1) Most German priests and lay people are in favour of a more pluriform type of priest than exists at present. (2) The clergy and the laity have very different views about the work of the clergy. (3) The lay person's image of the priest depends on the degree to which he practises—theological knowledge is valued more by the fully practising Catholic, an easy-going and sporting attitude by the "average" Catholic. (4) Catholics below the age of forty, both clergy and lay, have the greatest difficulty in accepting the traditional image of the priest. (This is a factor that emerges clearly from all the surveys.) Finally, (5) Germans are more reti-

---

[6] Some results can be found in *Synode, Amtliche Mitteilungen der Gemeinsamen Synode der Bistüme in der Bundesrepublik Deutschland* (1970–1972); see also "Die bundesdeutsche Priesterfrage", *Herder Korrespondenz* 25 (1971), pp. 383–7; the results of the German television inquiry have also been published in part: *Gegenwartsfragen der Kirche vor der Synode 1970, Repräsentativbefragung* (IFAK, Wiesbaden).

cent to accept the ordination of women than, for example, Canadians.

Austria

The crisis is clearly becoming more acute in Austria—20% fewer joined the priesthood in 1971 than in 1970. Even before the Roman Synod, the provisional results of a survey undertaken early in 1971 by the Austrian Institute for Religious Sociology (IKS) and answered by 74·2% of the clergy were discussed by the Austrian bishops who had commissioned the inquiry and were generally available in Austria.

Priests seemed on the whole remarkably satisfied with their situation, although many believed that there should be greater pluriformity, for example, married priests. The greatest difficulties encountered were loss of faith among the laity and uncertainty about the Church's teaching. Most priests found personal faith, prayer and study to be their greatest source of strength. It is clear from the survey that most older Austrian priests still have a traditional view of office, although the opinions of those below the age of thirty-two with regard to authority in the Church, married priests and so on were very different from those of the older clergy above the age of sixty-four.[7] Finally, the clergy is proportionately older than the rather ageing Austrian population.

Switzerland

The Swiss survey was initiated by the bishops, vicars general and eighteen delegates from the priests' councils and carried out by the Institute for Pastoral Sociology at St Gallen. All the diocesan priests were involved, but only a small number of regular priests, who were subsequently asked to co-operate in a separate inquiry in the Autumn of 1971. 84·8% of the 3,089 secular priests questioned responded to the first inquiry, which aimed to give them an opportunity to express their opinions about the problems confronting them and to ascertain their view of the priest's identity in a changing society and the difficulties involved. It is evi-

---

[7] Österreichische Priesterbefragung, Linearergebnisse (Institut für Kirchliche Sozialforschung, Vienna, 1971); "Die Priesterfrage aus österreichischer Sicht", Herder Korrespondenz 26 (1972), pp. 6–8.

dent from the provisional results that the majority of the clergy regard preaching and the sacraments as their main tasks, although 44% believe that the service of others is an essential part of the priest's mission. The majority are in favour of a secular occupation for the priest. Age and place of work—town or country—were decisive factors in determining opinion. Generally speaking, the results were similar to those obtained in the German survey.[8]

France

Apart from a non-scientific inquiry carried out at the request of the bishops, there has so far been no nation-wide survey, only limited surveys, for example, in the diocese of Metz,[9] in which priests and seminarists were questioned separately and in the diocese of Lille,[10] in which samples were taken among young people, militant Catholics and the laity generally to ascertain their image of the priesthood. There have been several studies of the attitude of younger Catholics towards the priesthood, illustrating clearly the phenomenon of the generation gap.[11]

The French bishops have also commissioned an interdisciplinary group to undertake a study of the priest, with special reference to the problem of celibacy,[12] but this survey is still in progress and no provisional results are yet available.

Spain

Without any doubt, the most important survey of the priest-

---

[8] *Die Schweizerische Priesterfrage* (Arbeitsbericht 2, 1968), *Der Pfarrerberuf* (Arbeitsbericht 7, parts 1 and 2, 1969–1971) and *Befragte Priester* (Arbeitsbericht 13, 1971), all published by the Institut Suisse de Sociologie Pastorale, St Gallen, which also prepared, with the Pastoralkommission der Vereinigung der Höhern Ordersobern der Schweiz, an inquiry among religious consisting of 174 questions, of which only the questionnaire is at present available. A detailed summary of the first results of the inquiry conducted among the secular clergy is available in "Die Schweizer Erhebung zur Priesterfrage", *Herder Korrespondenz* 25 (1971), pp. 515–19.

[9] *Sacerdoce et vocations*, two volumes, published by the Bureau d'Etudes socio-pastorales (Metz, n.d., stencilled).

[10] *Recherches sur le prêtre*, three reports published by the Centre Régional d'Etudes, socio-religieuses (Lille, 1970, stencilled).

[11] See, for example, the bibliography in "Western Youth and the Future of the Church", *Pro Mundi Vita* 33 (1970), pp. 26–7.

[12] Bureau d'Etude du Célibat sacerdotal (BECES); see *Le Monde*, 12 November 1971.

hood in Europe that has been completed is that carried out among the secular clergy in Spain in 1970 and 1971. This survey was preceded by a smaller, preliminary investigation among seminarists in 1968 and 1969;[13] it is worth noting that there was less than half the number of seminarists at the end of the decade 1961–1970 than at the beginning. The initiative was taken by the episcopal commissions for the clergy and for the seminaries and universities to carry out these surveys.

85% of the clergy answered the questionnaire, its 268 questions, the authors claimed, including every possible problem confronting the priest today, and the results were studied by an interdisciplinary team. What emerged very clearly was the extreme tension existing among Spanish priests with regard to their life in Spanish society, the teachings of Vatican II and the degree to which they have been assimilated, the problem of celibacy, the attitude of the hierarchy, the political situation and relationships between Church and State. A particularly acute problem in Spain is the critical attitude of young men towards the seminary system and their uncertainty about their vocations and about the identity of the priest generally. There is in Spain too a noticeable cleavage between the generations. On the positive side, many young priests and seminarists place their hopes in the increasing number of "post-conciliar" bishops.

Italy

Bishop Gaddi of Bergamo recently presented the Sixth General Assembly of bishops in Italy with a report based on a non-scientific survey in which 25,000 of the 43,000 diocesan priests had taken part, declaring that their greatest problems were loneliness and a low standard of living.[14] This finding has been confirmed by several scientific studies. S. Burgalessi[15] has provided a good synthesis of a number of regional surveys in which 3,700

[13] A detailed summary of both surveys has been published in "The Clergy and the Seminaries in Spain", *Pro Mundi Vita* 37 (1971). The survey among seminarists took place in 46 seminaries, 2,733 seminarists participating. Permission was refused in 24 seminaries, with about 2,000 students, to carry out the survey.

[14] *Il sacerdozio ministeriale. Problemi del clero in Italia* (Studium, 1970).

[15] S. Burgalessi, *Preti in Crisi? Tendenze sociologiche del clero italiano* (Fossano, 1970).

diocesan priests took part and a national survey in which 800 priests participated—altogether more than 10% of the Italian clergy. It is clear from these inquiries that Italian priests are in search of a new identity, that the crisis of faith is not identical with that of celibacy and that the crisis in the priesthood is closely connected with the crisis in society in general. Many priests in Italy, as in Spain, are very critical of the Church's leaders.

Other European Countries

Sociological surveys have either not been carried out in other countries in Europe or else their results have not been made public.[16] A confidential report on vocations was made in Ireland but not published. Surveys of limited scope have been undertaken in Yugoslavia, Malta and Hungary.[17] A clear though not scientific report of the situation has appeared in England.[18] The opinions of priests were sounded by the Scandinavian bishops with the 1971 Synod in mind[19] and a number of limited but fairly reliable opinion polls have been held in Belgium by priests' councils and the parish of the University of Louvain.[20]

THE UNITED STATES

Three great studies undertaken in America are cumulatively confirmatory. The first was carried out by J. H. Fichter of Harvard University at the request of a group of diocesan priests.[21] The second was conducted on the initiative of the National Federation of Priests' Councils by a team drawn from various

[16] A summary will be found in "Recent Evolution of Priestly Vocations. Confidential Note", *Pro Mundi Vita* 7 (1969).

[17] E. András, *Probleme der Priesterausbildung in Ungarn. UKI Berichte,* 3 (Vienna and Munich, 1970), pp. 3–21.

[18] *Official Report of the First National Conference of Secular Priests of England and Wales* (Wood Hall Centre, 1970).

[19] A representative sample test carried out among Danish Catholics to find their views about the priest (see *Informations Catholiques Internationales*, 1, 15 Jan. 1971, 10) came to the same conclusions as the Danish Synod, that is, in favour of pluriformity in the priesthood; see "The Dioesan Synod at Copenhagen. Special Note", *Pro Mundi Vita* 9 (1969).

[20] "The Priest in Search of his Identity. Special Note", *Pro Mundi Vita* 18 (1971), pp. 8–9.

[21] J. H. Fichter, *America's Forgotten Priests—What They Are Saying* (New York, 1968).

universities[22] in collaboration with the National Council of Churches, resulting in a comparison between the views of 8,000 Protestant pastors and 3,000 Catholic priests. The third was a large-scale survey undertaken by the American bishops' conference,[23] the sociological part of which was carried out by Chicago University.[24] Bishops, religious and ex-priests participated in this inquiry. The bishops' conference has been very reserved in its attitude towards the methods used and the results achieved,[25] but an episcopal commission is now (1972) working with experts with the aim of making recommendations on the basis of this survey. Three factors emerge very clearly from these American surveys—the almost universal experience of the generation gap, the problem of the conflict of authority and the difficulties involved in democratizing the Church.[26]

CANADA

In French-speaking Canada, social psychologists of Laval University have produced an outstanding study at the request of the bishops.[27] In English-speaking Canada, the priests themselves (National Federation of Priests' Senates) were the initiators, with the support of the bishops.[28] The most urgent problems confront-

[22] J. P. Koval and R. Bell, *A Study of Priestly Celibacy* (1971).

[23] The sociological survey forms part of a five volume study undertaken under the leadership of the Committee on Priestly Life and Ministry of the NCCB (American bishops' conference); the other volumes deal with history, psychology, Scripture and dogmatic theology.

[24] A. M. Greeley, *American Priests. A Report of the National Opinion Research Center* (Chicago, 1971).

[25] For Greeley's sharp criticism of the bishops' attitude, see A. M. Greeley, "The State of the Priesthood", *N.C.R. Documentation*, Supplement to the *National Catholic Reporter* (18 February 1971); see also *The Tablet* (26 February 1972).

[26] See also E. J. Schallert and J. M. Kelley, "Some Factors associated with Voluntary Withdrawal from the Catholic Priesthood", *Lumen Vitae* 25 (1970), pp. 425-60. E. Schallert, director of the Center for Sociological Research at San Francisco, questioned the official statistics concerning the number of priests in the U.S.A. in 1972 (58,000-60,000). He suggested 52,000 and possibly as few as 44,000 as a real total.

[27] P. Stryckman, *Les prêtres de Québec aujourd'hui*, I, published by the Centre de Recherches en Sociologie Religieuse, Université de Laval (Quebec, 1970); volume 2 is to be published in 1972.

[28] P. Stryckman and R. Gaudet, *Priests in Canada 1971. A Report on English-speaking Clergy*, published by the same centre (Quebec, 1971).

ing Canadian priests are celibacy and authority, together with
the tension arising from the open attitude of most priests and
their traditionally sacral appearance. In addition to the recurrent
problem of the generation gap, interesting similarities and differences between secular and regular clergy emerge from this
survey, together with the fact that very many priests are generally satisfied with their vocation. The same centre has also, at the
request of the National Office of the Clergy, which is also responsible for vocations, published a study on the attitude of students
towards priests.[29]

SOUTH AMERICA

On the basis of a number of scientific surveys,[30] the Brazilian
bishops have made their attitude towards a number of questions
concerning the priesthood clear.[31] A survey was carried out in
1968 by IBEAS among all Bolivian and foreign priests,[32] revealing serious differences between the two groups. The most search-
ing inquiry, however, was undertaken in Chile by R. Poblete of
the Centro Bellarmino.[33] About 60% of the clergy replied to this
survey, which dealt with all the important questions affecting
priests in the country. A clear need for fresh solutions to be found
for the pressing problems caused by the high percentage of foreign
missionaries was apparent from these surveys.[34]

AFRICA

The bishops of Zaire (formerly Congo-Kinshasa) conducted a

[29] J. P. Rouleau, *Le prêtre vu par étudiants de niveau collégial*, published
by the same centre (Quebec, 1971).
[30] "Brazil: The Church in Process of Renewal", *Pro Mundi Vita* 24
(1968); see also "Minas e Espirito Santo—Investigam o Ministério Sacerdotal", *Convergência* 38 (Sept. 1971), pp. 233 ff.
[31] "The National Episcopal Conference of Brazil regarding the Problem
of the Priesthood. Special Note", *Pro Mundi Vita* 8 (1969).
[32] Ponce García and O. Uzín Fernandez, "The Clergy in Bolivia. Special
Note", *Pro Mundi Vita* 11 (1970); this is a summary of *El Clero in Bolivia*,
published by IBEAS (La Paz, Bolivia, 1969, stencilled).
[33] *El Sacerdote Chileno. Estudio Sociologico*, published by the Centro
Bellarmino (Santiago de Chile, 1971, stencilled).
[34] "Foreign Priests in Latin America. Special Note", *Pro Mundi Vita* 15
(1970).

valuable non-scientific survey among their priests[35] and the results led to a number of decisions being made by the bishops in consultation with representatives of the clergy. The bishops of Rwanda and Burundi commissioned the centre CERES to carry out among all the clergy of both countries a survey, the three outstanding features of which proved to be the commonly experienced generation gap, differences in outlook between native and foreign priests and a strong desire for Africanization.[36] The results of a survey commissioned by the Ghanaian bishops will be published towards the end of 1972. In addition, several scientific surveys dealing with the work of catechists have been undertaken in Africa, the most notable being the study carried out by the Pastoral Institute at Gaba, Uganda, in the five countries of the East African bishops' conference (AMECEA) and the survey conducted in Rwanda and Burundi by CERES.[37]

ASIA AND AUSTRALASIA

No scientific surveys have as yet been completed in Asia, although one in which F. Houtart is collaborating is still in progress in Ceylon. No results of a serious study of the situation in South Korea have so far been published. Two Indian surveys—the first initiated by the priests of Kerala and the second by the bishops' conference—would appear to be non-scientific opinion polls. The results of surveys undertaken in Australia and New Zealand are not yet available.

SURVEYS AMONG RELIGIOUS AND MISSIONARIES

Most religious congregations and missionary institutes[38] are increasingly confronted with the need to change and some have carried out surveys among their members—for example, the

---

[35] "The General Consultation of African Secular Priests in Congo Kinshasa. Special Note", *Pro Mundi Vita* 16 (1971).

[36] *Recherche sur les prêtres. La vie et le ministère des prêtres*, four volumes published by CERES (Bujumbura).

[37] *Recherches Inter-africaine sur les Catéchistes*, published by CERES (Bujumbura, 1970, stencilled); A. Shorter and E. Katanza, *Missionaries to Yourselves. African Catechists Today* (London, 1972).

[38] "Missionary Institutes. Special Note", *Pro Mundi Vita* 12 (1970), provides a general review of fifteen missionary institutes.

Jesuits,[39] the Oblates and especially the Fathers of the Divine Word. Most of these studies are, however, not generally available.

CONCLUSION

The very fact that so many scientific surveys have been carried out so soon after the Second Vatican Council is in itself impressive from the sociological point of view. It is also a sign of the universal nature of the problems confronting office in the Church today, despite the obvious cultural differences between the groups questioned. It is also significant that not one sociological survey has been initiated by the Vatican itself.

There have, however, been very few surveys dealing with lay expectations of the priestly office, with new forms of office or with women in office or with the situation in other Churches regarding office. It would, in my opinion, be a very worthwhile task to study these possibilities scientifically. Similarly, very little has been done to investigate the situation in which the bishops and religious superiors find themselves today. Both from the point of view of sociological research and from that of pastoral theology, a survey or surveys carried out among the Church leaders, who are, after all, most affected by the current tensions in the Church, would seem to be very urgently required.

[39] T. M. Gannon, s.j., *Report on the Sociological Survey. North American Assistancy* (1970, stencilled).

Translated by David Smith

Marinus Houdijk

A Recent Discussion about the New Testament Basis of the Priest's Office

MY AIM in this article is simply to draw attention to the most important questions raised in the recent debate that has taken place in Germany about the New Testament basis of the priest's office in general and the priestly character of office in the Church in particular.

I. CRITICAL QUESTIONS ABOUT A SACRAL IMAGE OF THE PRIEST

At a congress held in September 1967 at Lucerne, "The Priest in the Secularized World", J. Blank questioned the sacral image of the priest on the basis of New Testament facts.[1] It is important to distinguish here between the priest as such and office in the Church as a *diakonia*, since Blank was not questioning the necessity of the latter. He was above all concerned with whether it was biblically justified to regard the priest as a sacral person with certain cultic functions which set him apart from the laity and with the historical assumption that the carrying out of those functions is the primary task of the priest. Blank pointed out firstly that there was originally no connotation of a sacral priesthood when the word "priest" (*presbyter*, elder) was used and secondly that the word "priest" (*hiereus, sacerdos*) was never applied in

---

[1] J. Blank, "Le prêtre à la lumière de la Bible", in *Bulletin d'Informations de l'Institut pour l'Entraide Sacerdotale en Europe*, 2 (1968), Nos. 1–2, pp. 19–36; this report is reprinted, somewhat abridged, in *Der Seelsorger*, 38 (1968), pp. 155–64. See also *idem*, "Kirchliches Amt und Priesterbegriff", in *Weltpriester nach dem Konzil* (Munich, 1969), pp. 11–52; *idem, Schriftauslegung in Theorie und Praxis* (Munich, 1969), pp. 60–71.

the New Testament to one holding office in the Church. In the New Testament, cultic or sacral terms were either avoided or else given a new meaning. For example, in his list of offices and services in the Church (1 Cor. 12. 27–30), Paul does not use the word "priest" at all and includes less important charisms without any hint of the division between office and charisms that exists today. In Phil. 1. 1, the *episkopoi*—in the plural, presumably as a "college"—and deacons are mentioned after the believers. Paul also used these terms in a non-sacral sense. In the gospels too, there is no indication that Jesus regarded the Twelve as a new priesthood.

How, then, could these New Testament functions (apostle, elder, teacher, *episkopos*, etc.) have become linked to terms and titles such as *sacerdos* and *pontifex*? It is probable that non-New Testament influences, for example, from Judaism, the pagan world and later medieval monasticism and clericalism, played a part in the Christian use of such terms. Thus, the successors of Peter could only have been given the title *sacerdos et pontifex* when the bishops had assumed the position that the pagan cultic functionaries had previously occupied from the time of Constantine onwards. It is therefore not that the essence of the New Testament office is not present in the priest, but rather that numerous elements unknown in the New Testament have gathered around that essence in the course of history. These non-New Testament elements have to be examined with care because they may stand in the way of a real renewal of office.

What is more, the reduction of the original pluriformity of offices and services to the episcopate, presbyterate and diaconate, the development of a hierarchy and the division into clergy and laity are also traceable, not to the New Testament, but to a tendency in the early Church to turn for inspiration to the hierarchical structure and the priesthood of the Old Testament. The Old Testament priesthood, however, was not exclusively a sacrificing priesthood—the prophets stressed the priest's task to spread knowledge about Yahweh, to instruct in the Torah and to preach the need for justice.

Jesus prayed and urged the need for prayer, but otherwise he was critical of all cultic acts (see, for example, Mark 12. 28–34; John 2. 14–22; 4. 21–24). His attitude towards the temple cult and the Jewish priesthood was also that of a prophet. For him, the whole of creation was the scene of God's activity with man, and obedience to God and his Word were worth more than all sacrifices. In going beyond the Jewish and pagan need for a cultic priesthood, he showed his opposition to a fundamental element in ancient civilization. His disciples too formed a "lay" community without any hierarchical structure. The Twelve are not seen in the New Testament as cultic priests, but as missionaries with the task of proclaiming the kingdom.

The Eucharist is not presented as a sacrifice in the New Testament and Jesus' association at table with his disciples and with sinners and the oppressed anticipates the universal community of man. Since it cannot therefore be compared with Jewish and pagan cultic and sacrificial institutions, we are bound to ask to what extent the Christian Eucharist should still be assimilated into an official cult with a sacred ritual and how far the leader in Christian worship should be a "priest".

Even in the Letter to the Hebrews, there is little trace of a sacerdotal function in the Church. The author regards Jesus as a high priest and his sacrificial death as the ultimate fulfilment of his total obedience to the Father's will, thus transcending all cult. He concludes his exposition of Jesus' high priesthood by quoting Ps. 40: "Sacrifices and offerings thou hast not desired, but a body thou hast prepared for me", a text summarizing the essentially critical role of the prophet (Heb. 10. 5–7). For Paul, Christ put an end to the law. For the author of Hebrews, he meant the end of all cultic and sacrificial priesthood—Christ's priesthood was above all eschatological.

The essential *diakonia* which ought to characterize every office in the Church and the multiplicity of the New Testament offices and services should act as guide-lines for any theology of priestly office rather than the way in which office has evolved since the second century A.D. Two different but not mutually exclusive developments are ascertainable in the New Testament. On the one hand, there is the Pauline type of community with its charismatic emphasis and, on the other, the Jewish Christian type as illustrated in Acts. Catholic theology and practice have given an almost exclusive emphasis on the Lucan model, despite the fact that Acts is not a faithful reproduction of early apostolic preach-

ing, and has to a great extent neglected the different conceptions of office and community not only in Paul, but also in
Matthew and John. The continued historical development of the
Lucan model does not necessarily mean that it is essentially cor-
rect. Our deeper understanding of the diversity of offices in the
New Testament and of the way in which later developments in
the Church have been historically conditioned and sociologically
determined make us ask inevitably which elements have been
given a one-sided emphasis and which can and should be stressed
now in a new situation. What is certain is that the Church's
offices and services or ministries should not, in the light of the
New Testament, be understood primarily as sacral, cultic or even
sacramental, but as functions of preaching and teaching.

II. THE PRIESTLY CHARACTER OF OFFICE IN THE CHURCH

We now turn to views about the priest's office in the New
Testament which are very different from those of Blank—the
views of Heinrich Schlier.[2] In so far as office and the people of
God are eschatological phenomena which cannot be fully grasped
by a purely historical and sociological approach, then office in
the Church has, in Schlier's opinion, a status which can only be
defined theologically. He believes that both the sacralization and
the profanization of the priest's office are based on a theological
misunderstanding and abuse of the priest's ministry which is
ultimately based on the unique priesthood of Christ. This type of
misunderstanding and abuse is partly attributable to prevailing
historical circumstances and political and social structures, but
what has, in Schlier's view, barely been acknowledged in the
recent discussion in Germany is that the priest's office has, by
virtue of its special origin, a distinctive structure in the Church
which can only be revealed by theology.

A purely historical investigation into the factual situation of
office in the New Testament can never, Schlier insists, fully re-

[2] H. Schlier, "Grundelemente des priesterlichen Amtes im Neuen Testament", in *Theologie und Philosophie*, 44 (1969), pp. 161–80; *idem*, "Die
neutestamentliche Grundlage des Priesteramtes", in *Der Priesterliche
Dienst*, 1 (Quaestiones Disputatae, 46) (Freiburg, Basle and Vienna, 1970),
pp. 81–114.

veal the essential character of office. Firstly, office was only at its initial stage of development in the New Testament and secondly this was itself only a historically conditioned realization of office and not its essential aspect. This can only be brought to light by a patient search for the fundamental principles which were active in the early realization of office in the New Testament and which have to some extent remained normative throughout the history of the Church.

The results of Schlier's study were integrated into the German bishops' letter on the priestly office which was published in 1969. The first part of this letter deals with the New Testament basis of the priest's office.[3] Stress is laid on the "fundamental" and "essential" aspects of office in the Church in order to provide a guide-line in the present debate. It is quite possible to distinguish an "objective continuity" of the "essential" aspect of office in the diversity of offices presented by the New Testament. The German bishops were aiming above all to provide a biblical justification of the Church's official priesthood. In their letter, then, they began by outlining certain basic principles governing office in the Church. Firstly, office was constituted by the authority of Jesus Christ, the three aspects of office being illuminated by Jesus' titles of king, prophet and priest. Secondly, it was derived from the office of apostle, the official character of the apostolate and the fact that the office-holder is placed "over and against" the community being visible in Paul's presentation of the apostolate. Quite early in the history of the Church, the authors of the letter maintain, certain offices developed from the apostolic office, but distinct from it. (Formal appointment to office and the sending out of those appointed are stressed in Acts by the imposition of hands and prayer.)

The primary tasks of these post-apostolic office-holders were preaching and teaching as well as the pastoral guidance of the community. The New Testament does not, it is true, state explicitly that they had a cultic or priestly character. It can, however, be demonstrated—and here the German bishops turn to the traditional argument—that this character is present theologically in the New Testament. Jesus' work of salvation is presented

[3] *Schreiben der deutschen Bischöfe über das priesterliche Amt. Eine biblisch-dogmatische Handreichung* (Trier, 1969).

in the New Testament primarily as priestly and these post-apostolic offices are a representation of Christ and are fundamentally related to the apostolic office.

The bishops also appeal to Hebrews to show that Christ's work of salvation was priestly. This is a relatively late theological reflection, but its basic elements concerning Christ's priesthood were already present in earlier writings, for example, Eph. 5. 2, where his "giving himself up for us" is called an "offering and sacrifice". According to Hebrews, this priesthood was unique, definitive and eschatological, making an end of all priesthood. The existence of a priestly office after Christ can only be justified on the basis of Christ's final and eternal priesthood. All the same, this later priesthood is certainly not merely symbolic, but real, just as, according to Hebrews, Christ's priesthood was real.

The German bishops also turn to Paul's justification of the apostolic office, in which he claims that he was called to be a minister to the Gentiles "in the priestly service of the gospel" (Rom. 15. 16). Paul saw his apostolic task here, the bishops argue, really and not merely symbolically as a priestly function, representing Christ's priestly work of salvation, and his total giving of himself in the service of the gospel made Christ's sacrifice visible, especially when he "shared in Christ's sufferings" (2 Cor. 1. 5).

The bishops naturally found it necessary to justify the cultic aspect of office in the Church which developed after the New Testament period. They freely admit that leading in eucharistic worship was not, in the New Testament, confined to those holding office, even to those holding apostolic office. But in Section 18 of the letter, in which Paul and the question of leading in the Eucharist are discussed, is a good illustration of the way in which the historical data are dealt with in this letter. On the one hand, the authors show a commendable openness in their definition of the historical situation. On the other hand, they order everything so that the later development of the cultic aspect of office is seen to emerge organically from the original data and, because of the "objective theological continuity" on which the authors insist, it is also seen to be binding.

Finally, although office in the Church has an essentially priestly character, the cultic and sacramental task is not, according to the bishops' letter, the only or even the primary function of the priest. Preaching the gospel and pastoral guidance of the community form an essential part of the priest's ministry.

III. No Harmonizing in Exegesis

W. Pesch[4] begins his article by pointing to an error commonly made by authors who deal with this subject, that of tracing later developments in the Church unquestioningly back to the New Testament. An example of this is the assumption that a priest led in the worship of the Corinthian community. Such attempts to "harmonize" are wrong—the exegete cannot, Pesch insists, make the New Testament say more than it does in fact say. He must realize that there is no clear teaching about the priesthood or the basic elements of office either in Paul or in the New Testament as a whole. There are only occasional statements, often difficult to reconcile with each other and even contradictory, made by different theologians in different writings for different communities. The exegete has to accept these differences.

This problem has not, Pesch thinks, been resolved in the German bishops' letter. Although the letter does not obscure the historical situation of the New Testament and is open to other possible forms of office in the future, its aim is above all to justify the factual development in the Church and the established pattern of ecclesiastical office. The activity of the Holy Spirit cannot be confined to the Church of the past. While looking for the "essential" aspects of office in the New Testament, the exegete must also be conscious of the possibility of gaining a deeper insight into that activity in the Church of the present and the future.

The exegete, Pesch believes, has to examine critically statements that have traditionally been interpreted as favouring the priestly character of office. Paul's presentation of his ministry to proclaim the gospel as a "priestly" liturgical activity (Rom. 15. 16) is, for example, a bold image. Paul did not see himself as a priest. The very opposite is true—he was doing away with "priestly" activity by degrading it to the level of a mere image

---

[4] W. Pesch, "Priestertum und Neuen Testament", *Trierer Theologische Zeitschrift*, 79 (1970), pp. 63–83.

of his "unpriestly" activity. His use of the terminology of sacrifice in Phil. 2. 17 is similar in that he was in this passage discussing Christian realities which were not included within a cultic or sacerdotal framework. What is more, Paul was the only apostle who used such "priestly" images. (In Acts, it should be noted, he was not recognized as an apostle.) Moreover, because he had no knowledge of a "priestly" Christology, it would be mistaken to try to "harmonize" his statements with the later theology of Hebrews. The priestly Christology of Hebrews occupies a special place, quite distinct from the rest of the New Testament, in which Jesus is never called a priest. Other cultic terms used elsewhere in the New Testament and statements about Jesus' giving of himself (Mark 10. 45; 14. 24; Luke 22. 19) should not be regarded as veiled references to the priestly character of Jesus' work of salvation, but rather as images or as quotations.

There are many cases in the Jewish literature of the first century A.D. describing the Old Testament priesthood as a foreshadowing of the expected Messiah and, although we do not know the precise sources used by the author of Hebrews, we may assume that he was in this tradition. What really distinguishes Hebrews is its emphasis on the unique character of Jesus' work of salvation. The author was alone among the New Testament writers in regarding the Old Testament priesthood as a foreshadowing of the unique and definitive priesthood of Christ. His intention was clearly to impress on the community of believers that they had to abandon the purely cultic sphere and belong exclusively to the Lord, whose work of salvation was not at an end. As Bishop H. Volk has correctly pointed out, the character of Jesus' priesthood is so distinctive that we have no need to call him a priest.[5] The method and the imagery used in the priestly Christology of Hebrews are full of contradictions and we should be careful of quoting the letter in our attempts to justify the priestly character of office, especially when the letter seems to recognize its existence (the "leaders" of Heb. 13. 7, 17, 24) without linking it with Christ's priestly office. The author himself probably did not intend this.

The exegete has also, Pesch is convinced, to be critical of any

[5] H. Volk, "Der Priester und sein Dienst. Zum Schreiben der deutschen Bischöfe über das priesterliche Amt", in *Publik*, 3 (1970), No. 1, pp. 23-4.

attempt to derive the priestly character of office in the Church from the New Testament title "priestly people of God". The texts referring to the universal priesthood of all believers are concerned only with certain tasks which are summarized as "spiritual sacrifices" (1 Pet. 2. 5) and only express the close bond existing between these believers and Christ. There is no justification for the assumption that there was a cultic or sacrificial "priesthood" of believers. There is no evidence of this anywhere in the New Testament and, when cultic terms are found in the New Testament, they should as it were be placed between inverted commas. The texts in 1 Pet. certainly do not refer to a cultic celebration of the Eucharist, for example, nor does 1 Pet. 5. 1–3 suggest that the leaders of the community had a priestly function.

Pesch therefore concludes that priority must be given to the proclamation of the gospel in the widest sense because of the fundamentally apostolic character of office in the New Testament. We must also fully accept the multiplicity of offices and services or ministries in the New Testament in any attempt to understand "priesthood" in the light of the biblical data and examine what possible forms of office in the future are suggested by the New Testament. It is, for example, possible to recognize *within* the Lucan model and that of the Pastoral Letters that the community may play a part in appointing those to hold office and that the presbyterate may function collectively, like the episcopate and the diaconate elsewhere. Women should perhaps be given official status in the service of the Church on the basis of the New Testament office of widows. The office of teacher, in other words, of "theologian", is also present alongside that of shepherd or pastor in Hebrews and other texts.

IV. The Old Testament Priesthood

N. Lohfink[6] has stressed the importance of a study of the Old Testament priesthood as a means of solving the problems of the priesthood today. A clear distinction should be made, he insists, between two different levels of meaning contained in our

[6] N. Lohfink, "Das Alte Testament und die Krise des kirchlichen Amts", in *Stimmen der Zeit*, 185 (1970), pp. 269–76.

use of the word "priest". At the first level, that of sociology, the priest is a functionary whose services are the necessary consequence of natural and sociological laws which become effective as soon as men begin to live in a religious society or a Church. It is obvious, then, that a comparison can be made at this level between a religious society such as ancient Israel and the Church. At the second level, that of theology, there are the Christological statements in the New Testament about Christ's high priesthood and sacrificial death and especially about his doing away with the Old Testament priesthood. It is clear that these are to be understood not in a sociological sense, but in a figurative sense and we should therefore not draw sociological or ecclesiological conclusions from them.

An example of the type of illogical thinking that can result from the confusion of these two levels: In the theological sense, Jesus was priest, king and prophet at the same time, although three distinct functions were implied in the original sociological sense in which these terms were used in ancient Israel. The identification of these three originally distinct offices in the one person of Christ is proof that they were no longer understood in the New Testament in the purely sociological sense. Is it right, then, to adhere to this theological identification when we turn to the sociological question of office or offices in the Church today?

This is in fact what is done when it is stressed that the offices of priest, pastor and teacher have always to be united in one person because the one office-bearer is the representative of Christ. But has this representative necessarily to represent Christ in every respect? Those who defend the historical development which has led to the priestly, pastoral and prophetic functions being concentrated in the one person of the priest usually resort to the argument that the three functions flow from each other and essentially require each other. The inherent fallacy of this argument can be seen at once if the three terms are examined. In the Old Testament, a sharp distinction is made between the priest, the shepherd and the prophet and the three functions were seldom united in one person; when that happened it was purely accidental.

All this goes to show, then, how dangerous it can be to apply the New Testament priestly Christology to the problem of the priest's office in the Church today, which is ultimately more sociological than theological. Lohfink therefore suggests that the Old Testament is a better guide because of its abundance of models for different functions and changes in those functions within the concept of office and because its idea of the "priest" was so flexible.

V. The Image of the Shepherd

H. Urs von Balthasar[7] has attempted to define the priesthood by appealing to the image of the shepherd that runs through the whole of Scripture. God appeared as a shepherd to the people of the Old Testament and chose from among them shepherds who proclaimed his word and embodied in their lives his pastoral care of the people. The New Testament continued this tradition and gave it an eschatological emphasis in the person of Christ. In the Church too, the priesthood has traditionally been characterized by the biblical image of the shepherd.

We may conclude by saying that this image is especially valuable in that it includes the original idea of opposition and reciprocity, the shepherd being placed "over and against" his flock. Both in ordinary and in religious usage, the image also has a predominantly ethical and existential content and implies care of, responsibility for and commitment to one's brothers (1 John 3. 16).

[7] H. Urs von Balthasar, "Der Priester im Neuen Testament. Eine Ergänzung", in *Geist und Leben*, 43 (1970), pp. 30-45.

Translated by David Smith

Biographical Notes

JOAN BROTHERS was born in Liverpool in 1938 and studied at the University there. Doctor of sociology, she is lecturer in sociology at Goldsmiths' College, London University. She has given lectures on sociological themes (especially on the possible relation between sociology and theology) in many Protestant and Catholic institutions; she is engaged on the reclassification of ancient members of the secular clergy; she has taken part in many ecumenical activities (particularly in dialogues arranged by the World Council of Churches). Among her published works are: *Church and School: A Study of the Impact of Education on Religion* (Liverpool, 1964), *Readings in the Sociology of Religion* (Oxford, 1969²), *The Uses of Sociology* (with J. D. Halloran) (London, 1966), *Residence and Student Life* (with S. R. Hatch) (Tavistock, 1971) and *Religious Institutions* (London, 1971).

JEAN COLSON was born 13 September 1913 in Menil en Xaintois (France) and ordained in 1938. He studied in Paris at the Institut Catholique and the Sorbonne. Doctor of theology, he has been professor of the history of the origins of Christianity at the Faculty of Theology of Angers since 1961 and attached to the Centre d'études du Secours Catholique Français. Among his principal published works are: *Ministre de Jésus-Christ ou le Sacerdoce de l'Evangile, L'énigme du disciple que Jésus aimait, Prêtre et peuple sacerdotal, L'évêque dans les communautés primitives, L'épiscopat catholique: Collégialité et Primauté dans les trois premiers siècles de l'Eglise, Les Fonctions ecclésiales aux deux premiers siècles, La Fonction diaconale aux origines de l'Eglise, Clément de Rome*, and *Paul Apôtre Martyr*.

PIET FRANSEN, s.j., was born 10 December 1913 in Tournai and was ordained in 1943. He studied at St Jean Berchmans College, Louvain and at the Gregorian University, Rome. Doctor of theology and licentiate in philosophy, he is (since 1969) professor of theological anthropology at Louvain University and editor-in-chief (for Belgium) of the review *Bijdragen*. Among his published works are: *Grenade, Werkelijkheid en Leven* (Antwerp, 1959) and a series of articles in *Intelligent Theology* (London and Chicago, 3 vols., 1967, 1968, 1969).

ALEXANDRE GANOCZY was born in Budapest in 1928. He studied at the Pázmány University of Budapest, at the Institut Catholique, Paris, and at the Gregorian University, Rome. Doctor of theology and of philosophy, he is consultor to the Secretariat for the Union of Christians and professor of systematic theology at the University of Würzburg. Among his published works are: *Calvin, théologien de l'Eglise et du ministère* (Paris, 1964), *Le jeune Calvin* (Wiesbaden, 1966) and *Ecclesia ministrans* (Freiburg im B., 1968). He has also contributed articles to *Concilium, Recherches de Science Religieuse, Geist und Leben, Theologische Revue*, etc.

MARINUS HOUDIJK was born 11 June 1936 in Gouda (Netherlands). He studied philosophy and theology at the Major Seminary of Warmond (Netherlands) and obtained the title of doctorandus in theology at the Faculty of Theology of Nijmegen, where he has worked since 1967 as a scientific assistant.

PETER KEARNEY was born 16 September 1935 in New York City and was ordained in 1959. A licentiate in Holy Scripture (Pontifical Biblical Institute, Rome), he is assistant professor of Holy Scripture at the Catholic University of America, Washington, D.C. He wrote "Joshua" for *The Jerome Biblical Commentary* (1968).

JAN KERKHOFS, S.J., was born 15 May 1924 in Hasselt (Belgium) and was ordained in 1956. He studied at the Jesuit Faculty of Theology in Louvain and at the Universities of Louvain and Oxford. Licentiate in philosophy and in theology, doctor of sociology, he is general secretary of "Pro Mundi Vita" and professor of pastoral sociology at the Faculty of Theology of Louvain University.

RENÉ LAURENTIN was born 19 October 1917 in Tours and ordained in 1946. He studied at the Institut Catholique, Paris, and at the Sorbonne. Docteur ès lettres, doctor of theology, he is professor of theology at the Catholic University of Angers and teaches in many universities: in Canada (Montreal, Quebec), in the U.S.A. (Dayton) and in Latin America, etc. He was consultor to the Preparatory Theological Commission of Vatican II and then an official expert at the Council. He is responsible for the religious chronicle of the journal *Le Figaro* (Paris) and carries on a pastoral ministry in the neighbourhood of Paris. Among his numerous published works, many of which deal with questions of Mariology and Vatican II, are: *Développement et salut, Noveaux ministères et fin du clergé, Réorientation de l'Eglise après le troisième Synode, Lourdes: Documents authentiques* (6 vols.), *La Vierge au Concile, Jésus et le Temple, Dieu est-il mort?, Crise et promesse d'Eglise aux USA, Nouvelles dimensions de l'espérance*. He edits the Mariological chronicle in *La Revue des Sciences Philosophiques et Theologiques*.

ANDRÉ LEMAIRE was born 2 January 1942 in Neuville (France) and ordained in 1966. He studied at the Institut Catholique, Paris, at the Biblical School of Jerusalem and at the Ecole Pratique des Hautes Etudes (Sciences Religieuses), Paris. After being chaplain to students, he is now professor of Holy Scripture at the Centre d'Etude et de Réflexion Chrétienne in

Orleans and assistant lecturer at the Faculty of Theology of Paris. His most important published work is *Les ministères au origines de l'Eglise, naissance de la triple hiérarchie: évêques, presbytres, diacres* (Paris, 1971).

Right Rev. STEPHEN NEILL was born 31 December 1900 in Edinburgh. He is a member of the Anglican Church, in which he was ordained priest in 1928 and consecrated bishop in 1939. He studied at Trinity College, Cambridge (M.A.). He is a member of the British Academy and a doctor *honoris causa* of five universities, was Bishop of Tinnevelly (India) 1939–45 and Auxiliary Bishop of Canterbury 1949–50. He was professor of missions and of ecumenical theology at the University of Hamburg 1962–67 and is now professor of philosophy and of religious studies at the University of Nairobi. Among his published works (more than 30 books) are: *A Genuinely Human Existence* (1959), *The Interpretation of the New Testament* (1964), *A History of Christian Missions* (1965), *Colonialism and Christian Missions* (1967), *The Church and Christian Union* (1968), *Christianity in India and Pakistan* (1970), *Bible Words and Christian Meanings* (1970), *What do you know of Jesus?* (1970).

FRANZ SCHNIDER was born 7 July 1937 in Entetswil (Switzerland) and ordained in 1965. He studied Catholic theology at Lucerne and Fribourg and biblical sciences in Rome and Jerusalem. He is assistant professor of New Testament exegesis at the Faculty of Catholic Theology of the University of Regensburg. He has written, in collaboration with Werner Stenger, *Die Ostergeschichten der Evangelien* (Munich, 1970) and *Johannes und die Synoptiker: Vergleich ihrer Parallelen* (Munich, 1971).

WERNER STENGER was born 14 November 1938 in Bad Kreuznach (Germany) and ordained in 1963. He studied Catholic theology at Innsbruck, Munich and Trèves. He is assistant professor of New Testament exegesis at the Faculty of Catholic Theology at the University of Regensburg. For his published works, see previous entry (Schnider).